W9-BBR-883

CHICAGO
COMEDY

CHICAGO
COMEDY
A FAIRLY SERIOUS HISTORY

MARGARET HICKS
Foreword by Mick Napier

THE
History
PRESS

Published by The History Press
Charleston, SC 29403
www.historypress.net

Copyright © 2011 by Margaret Hicks
All rights reserved

Cover design by Natasha Momberger

First published 2011

ISBN 978.1.60949.211.3

Library of Congress Cataloging-in-Publication Data

Hicks, Margaret, 1970-
Chicago comedy : a fairly serious history / Margaret Hicks.
p. cm.
Includes bibliographical references and index.
ISBN 978-1-60949-211-3
1. Stand-up comedy--Illinois--Chicago--HIstory. 2. Comedians--Illinois--Chicago--
Biography. 3. Theater--Illinois--Chicago--History. 4. Improvisation (Acting) 5. Music-halls
(Variety-theaters, cabarets, etc.)--Illinois--Chicago--History. 6. Radio comedies--Illinois-
-Chicago--History and criticism. 7. Television comedies--Illinois--Chicago--History and
criticism. I. Title.
PN1969.C65H53 2011
792.709773'11--dc22
2011009606

Notice: The information in this book is true and complete to the best of our knowledge. It is
offered without guarantee on the part of the author or The History Press. The author and
The History Press disclaim all liability in connection with the use of this book.

All rights reserved. No part of this book may be reproduced or transmitted in any form
whatsoever without prior written permission from the publisher except in the case of brief
quotations embodied in critical articles and reviews.

R0456093958

We struck the home trail now, and in a few hours were in the astonishing Chicago—a city where they are always rubbing the lamp, fetching up the genii, and contriving and achieving new possibilities.

—*Mark Twain,* Life on the Mississippi

CONTENTS

FOREWORD

I feel very fortunate in the world of comedy. I have worked with some of the most intelligent and funniest people in the last quarter of a century. All in Chicago.

When I was attending Indiana University in the early 1980s, I had never heard of improvisation. I was studying theater and was growing weary of rehearsing the same thing over and over and over. I stumbled upon Jeffery Sweet's *Something Wonderful Right Away.* Well, I guess that changed my life. Theater could be different every time you walked on stage. The comedy show could change from night to night. You could make it up as you go along. So I started an improv group in college, having never seen or performed it. Now, twenty-five years later, having founded the Annoyance Theatre and performed, taught and directed numerous shows for the Second City, I truly have worked with the funniest people in the United States.

I remember the first Second City main stage show I directed. I was sitting in the middle of the theater, and I had the cast on stage improvising. It was probably one o'clock in the afternoon. I thought to myself, "How is it that I have managed to have the main stage cast of the Second City perform for me alone in the afternoon?" I felt scared and privileged. I'm also privileged to have worked with and met the very founders of modern American improvisation, and I'm proud to have been a part of and influenced it myself.

When you endeavor to learn about Chicago's comedy history, you can't ignore the history of Chicago itself. Chicago's culture, politics, weather, geography, industry and people create a comedy environment that is, for lack of a better word, real. Really fearless. Really honest. Really funny. It's a city where you can create comedy that fails. It's a city where you can create comedy that kills. It's a city where you can hone your craft, like no other city in America. It's always been a city that could use a good laugh.

It's an honor to introduce you to this wonderful journey into the history of comedy in Chicago. Enjoy.

Mick Napier

ACKNOWLEDGEMENTS

This has been such an amazing process. I'd like to thank everyone who ever walked the earth, really, but no one wants to read all those names. I get that.

Thank you to the generous people I interviewed for this book: Brian Babylon, Aaron Freeman, Dave Gaudet, Bert Haas, Don Hall, Charna Halpern, Joe Janes, Susan Messing, Sheldon Patinkin, Jonathan Pitts, Bernie Sahlins, Scott Siegel, Tim Samuelson, Mark Sutton and Tom Tenney.

Thank you to the lovely people who helped me gather photographs: Doug Diefenbach, John Eiberger, Fuzzy Gerdes, Charna Halpern, Angela Manginelli, Ken Manthey, Jonathan Pitts and Jerry Schulman.

And to the supporting cast: Thank you to my husband for the continuous supply of gummy bears. Also, Winston's Café deserves a thank you for letting me sit there for hours to write. And to my friends and family, my nearest and dearest, who supported me throughout the whole thing.

But most of all, thank you to Chicago. You big beautiful city you.

INTRODUCTION

The history of Chicago comedy is a big subject. When I first mentioned to Mick Napier that I was going to write a book on the history of Chicago comedy, he looked me dead in the eyes and said, "That's a big book." He's not kidding. If I could even document all the movements that made up the history of Chicago comedy—all the bits, edits, radio shows, TV shows, comedians, improvisers—I would be writing forever. It's an enormous subject.

Even trying to comprehend my own personal history in this community is a monumental project. I've seen hundreds of improv shows and dozens and dozens of stand-ups and met thousands of people, all with a voice and something to say. And that is just my history. Once I start thinking about everyone who came before me and all the shows they saw, all the people they met, it's a staggering amount of information.

Yet what amazed me in writing this book were all the similarities. All those people, all those stories—and still, we all have so much in common. If comedy is in your blood, then that's half the battle. Chicago becomes a place to express yourself.

My own history started at the Improv Comedy Club, which used to be located in River North. I had always wanted to work there; it was my secret wish. In a divine stroke of luck, I landed an interview to work in the box office. When I walked into that huge club, where I had been a customer so many times before, it blew me away. It was so big, so airy. It felt so different during the daytime. It was quiet, peaceful—almost like a church. I could feel the energy of a thousand comedians glowing through their pictures on the wall. I was in awe. My potential boss (who incidentally became one of the best friends I've ever known) interviewed me on the stage, in front of that famous brick wall. That moment is still up there as one of the greatest times of my life.

Needless to say, I got the job.

My first real class was at iO a few years later. I needed something to do. I needed new friends. I had seen *Whose Line Is It Anyway*, and like so many improvisers who were inspired by that show, I thought, "I can do that." And the first day I walked into class was the day I made the best friends of my life. I had the strongest sense of "So this is where all my people are!" They're still my best friends today.

I've performed all over the city, in various groups with punny names. I've performed on stages, in bars and even outside on the grass for fifty kids who couldn't have cared less. I'm old school now; I've been around for a long time, and I have not begun to scratch the surface of all the comedy there is to see in Chicago.

So please, I beg your pardon if I've missed a favorite comedian of yours or something that, in your mind, changed it all. Trust me, I've fit in as much as I can, and my mission for you is to get out there and experience it—taste of Chicago's finest export. And you might want to do that now because everything will be different tomorrow.

1

A HISTORY LESSON

Chicago will give you a chance. The sporting spirit is the spirit of Chicago.
—Lincoln Steffens

It's hard to imagine now, what with buildings that scrape the sky and elevated trains that rumble high overhead, but Chicago was an unlikely place for a city. It had no plan, no particular destiny. It wasn't until it was experienced and molded by men that this land held any fate. Take away the buildings, the boats and the miles of railroad lines and imagine instead a swampy bog inhabited by a few Native Americans. In the warm months, Indians did their fur trading up and down the river that wound its way through the prairie. In the cold months, even the Indians would skip town. The howling winter winds would shoot across the color-stripped plains, and in summer, the prairie grass would sway in the lake breeze. This breeze carried the scent of a foul-smelling onion the Indians called *checagou*—and with that, Chicago was born with a joke on its lips. A global city known for its architecture, business and big shoulders was named after a particularly smelly onion. Good one Chicago, good one.

The first white men to come to Chicago were two Frenchmen sent by the governor of France to explore new lands for expansion. Father Jacques Marquette and Louis Jolliet arrived here from Green Bay in 1674. They were impressed with the abundance found on the prairie land. Bison roamed free, and the soil grew corn and wheat easily. As Marquette and Jolliet made their way back to France—probably thinking about Chicago, "Meh, it was *okay*"—the two men were shown a shortcut, a portage that linked the Great Lakes with the Mississippi River. Anywhere a canoe could be carried to connect two waterways was precious. Water was transportation, and transportation meant business; thus, a portage was a valuable asset. Both Marquette and Jolliet knew they had found an important spot, a spot that shivered and shook with the anticipation of growth. Once home, Jolliet pressed the French to build a canal to create a direct waterway between the Illinois and Mississippi Rivers, a canal that would connect east to west. Alas, the canal would not be built by the French.

Jolliet had seen the seed of Chicago's power, and this was all that was needed to spark the fire. Chicago was obscure no more. Only nine years after Jolliet and Marquette, another French explorer, Robert Cavelier de La Salle, began to map the land, and he too saw, perhaps better than anyone, a destiny for the invisible city:

> *This will be the gate of empire, this the seat of commerce. Everything invites to action. The typical man who will grow up here must be an enterprising man. Each day as he rises he will exclaim, "I act, I move, I push," and there will be spread before him a boundless horizon, an illimitable field of activity.*[1]

The first permanent settler was Jean Baptiste Pointe du Sable, a French-Haitian black man who built his house at the mouth of the Chicago River about 1770. He made his living trading furs and goods with the Indians and the few travelers in the area. Generally, it was a quiet, if cold, existence. In 1804, Fort Dearborn, Chicago's first permanent structure, was built at the corner of modern-day Wacker and Michigan Streets. Fort Dearborn was all about the portage; the Americans were catching on to its possibilities, and the fort was built to protect the portage from the Indians. In 1812, after a bloody attack, Fort Dearborn was burned and then rebuilt in 1816. In 1818, Illinois was incorporated as a state, and by 1837, the year of Chicago's incorporation as a city, this tiny, fur-trading spot had grown in population to roughly four thousand people, mostly French and French-Indians plying their trades on the lethargic and lazy river.

The early days of Chicago were harsh ones. It was not easy to live on this hostile land. Settlers were isolated from much of the world and living without the rules and laws of polite society. Still populated by a racy mix of French and Indian traders, the only real relief from the elements came in the disguise of the local saloon. Chicago's first entrepreneur was a man named Mark

Chicago in its early stages. The Sauganash Hotel can be seen in the foreground. *Photo courtesy of the Chicago History Museum.*

Beaubien, who built the Sauganash Hotel on Wolf Point at the confluence of the north and south branches of the Chicago River. Although it sounds like a respectable place, the Sauganash was "an impressive structure in the town, it was more of a frontier tavern with rooms above it than the eastern image of a hotel."[2] Mark Beaubien was the epitome of an early Chicagoan; "to old settlers, he was 'our Beaubien,' part civilized, part savage in spirit, a reckless but lovable man who managed to spend whatever he made."[3] Soon, Beaubien, father of a whopping twenty-three children, found he was flush enough to open a saloon next to his hotel. Men and women—because all were welcome in this lawless frontier town—went to the Sauganash to drink and dance. White men danced with Indian women, and drink was plentiful. The Sauganash was a rowdy place, and its most sophisticated form of entertainment consisted of Mr. Beaubien pulling out his fiddle and playing a rollicking song for his patrons. Sometimes, just to mess with the easterners, white men would dress up as Indians and enter the saloon hollering and hooting, scaring the big apple right out of those New Yorkers.

As Chicago grew, so did its relationship with New York City. New York was a much older city; its first colonies were settled in 1624 by the Dutch. New York had strong ties to Chicago and wanted and needed it to do well.

In *City of the Century*, Donald Miller notes, "New York, the busiest ocean harbor in the world, and Chicago, the busiest inland harbor in the world, became linked by nature and man, their economic destinies intertwined. Throughout the nineteenth century, as Chicago prospered, so did New York; and vice versa."[4] Land grabbing in Chicago was at an all-time high. Men could make fortunes in a matter of minutes. Easterners were coming to buy and sell land in the town, so their profits were linked to the success of the land they purchased. It was important Chicago succeeded. The relationship with New York would continue as not only a bane to Chicago's existence but a boon to it as well. New Yorkers brought their eastern ways with them, and in the case of Mark Beaubien, the arrival of easterners forced his early exit. He left for Naperville claiming he had to leave Chicago because he "didn't expect no town."[5]

As New Yorkers spilled into the lawless city of Chicago, they yearned for more culture than Chicago could offer. Devoid of theaters but flush with saloons, proper entertainment in Chicago was difficult to find. New Yorkers had grown used to paying for and enjoying the refined theaters of New York City, but Chicago was still so young and base that its residents showed their love for performance by yelling and banging on tables at the Sauganash. There were a few performances by traveling entertainers who made their way to Chicago, usually one-man shows that specialized in a variety of fascinating spectacles for the audience. On February 24, 1834, the first performance that required actual payment was held in the private home of Dexter Graves. A Mr. Bowers was to arrive and "introduce many very amusing feats of Ventriloquism and Legerdemain, many of which are original and too numerous to mention…Performance to commence at early candlelight."[6]

Chicagoans learned early on that a sense of humor was essential to living in a struggling frontier town in 1834. As Chicago's population increased, the muddy streets became a hazard. Farmers and horses both would get stuck in the knee-deep mud that arrived every spring. Huge holes would appear where horses and wagons were dug up out of the mud. Chicago's first comedians left signs saying, "No Bottom Here" or "The Shortest Road to China."

2

THE SAVAGE TAMED

I have struck a city—a real city—and they call it Chicago...I urgently desire never to see it again. It is inhabited by savages.
—Rudyard Kipling, American Notes

It is important when talking about the history of Chicago comedy to start with the theaters that made their home in the city. Since very few people actually settled in this frontier town, it was the theater managers who dictated style and form. Individual performers came from all over, often passing through from other small towns. Specific performers are hard to track considering they had stage names and were never in town for long, blowing out as the winter winds blew in.

A few years after Chicago's incorporation in 1837, the first permanent theater group arrived—no doubt the influence of easterners searching for a new place of entertainment. The new theater group called itself the Chicago Theater. Mr. Harry Isherwood, the founder of the group, came to Chicago to see if it was a suitable place to open his new theater. But unlike the hopeful words of La Salle, Isherwood's words conveyed his shock at the state of the frontier town:

In 1837 I arrived in Chicago, at night, and was driven to a hotel in the pelting rain. The next morning it was still raining. Went out to take a view of the place. A plank road, about three feet wide, was in front of the building. I saw to my astonishment a flock of quail on the plank.

I returned to my hotel, disappointed at what I saw of the town, and made up my mind that this was no place for a show.[1]

Yet Isherwood and his partner, Alexander McKenzie, stayed and housed the Chicago Theater group in the dining room of the vacated Sauganash Hotel. They put on a few plays like *The Idiot Witness*, a comedic melodrama; *The Stranger*; and *The Carpenter of Rouen*. The bill would change every night, as Chicago audiences weren't patient enough to have it any other way. After six weeks, the company went on tour, and when it came back in 1838, it made its new home in the Rialto.

The Rialto was "a den of a place, looking more like a dismantled grist-mill than a temple of anybody."[2] It wasn't a fancy theater; in fact, it was originally an auction house named for the part of town where it was located. It had four walls and flimsy wood—not so different from the small, independent theaters of today. But no matter, Isherwood and McKenzie worked with what they had and added a gallery and a pit to create a real theater experience. The four-hundred-seat theater changed its name to the Chicago Theater, no doubt a more cosmopolitan name than the Rialto. Isherwood and McKenzie did their best to bring an air of sophistication to the city. Instead of hiring the variety acts normally seen in saloons, they put on scripted plays, a practice many of the new elite found more appropriate.

The new culture emerging in Chicago saw drama as a serious undertaking to be experienced in a proper theater. But comedy, the hedonistic art form that it was, was relegated to the saloons. Women used to dance and sing along with the men in the old days of the Sauganash, but that was no more. Women appearing in saloons was frowned upon now. Men would go to the saloons for a respite from the hardscrabble days of battling a new frontier and, more likely, to get away from their wives. To the saloons they would go for their nightly liquor and ladies of the night. To keep the men entertained, variety performers of all sorts would play instruments, tell jokes and sing songs. Tim Samuelson, city historian, says:

There are references to people who had routines where they would dress up as a character or come out and do observations also combined with music. It's not like the divisions of what kind of performer you were were really clean. Even the people who performed would often combine things, so you would get up and make an observation about the time or politics and then break into a song[3]

The men of Chicago would let it be known if they liked a show by throwing their money on stage—or fruit if they didn't. And in a move that would reverberate for the next 150 years, many of the men would participate in the show, running up on stage or influencing the show from the audience. Chicagoans always let it be known what they thought of their local theater, and from then on, the actors on stage began to listen.

Isherwood and McKenzie wanted to stay away from the base comedy being performed at the bars; they wanted to attract the new elite. They found it helpful to put on shows that were already popular in New York. Theater managers in Chicago also employed "stock stars"—actors who were well known around the country. These stock stars began to populate Chicago's theaters and gave the theater scene a boost in respectability. Although these stock stars tended to eat up money that Chicago certainly didn't have, the city wished to present itself as grown up. If Chicago liked what New York already adored, then it was on the right track.

A young family of actors by the name of Jefferson traveled with Isherwood and McKenzie. Joseph and Cornelia Jefferson arrived in Chicago with their daughter and nine-year-old son. Upon arriving, Joseph Jr. described Chicago as "a busy little town, busy even then, people hurrying to and fro, frame buildings going up, board sidewalks going down, new hotels, new churches, new theaters, everything new."[4] Joseph Jr. learned quickly how to entertain the audience members so they would throw coins in appreciation. Isherwood and McKenzie used the boy to fill out scenes or add a comic song to a particularly long drama. Joseph became quite adept at the stage and later in life became one of the great comedic actors of his time, known mostly for his roles as the gravedigger in *Hamlet* and his impression of Rip Van Winkle. Joseph Jefferson's name is immortalized in the annual Joseph Jefferson Awards, Chicago's version of the Tony Awards.

Isherwood and McKenzie were reasonably successful in Chicago, but they found that the winter months made it impossible to be profitable. Chicago's measly four thousand people weren't enough to sustain a permanent theater. They were losing money, and the traveling circuit called to them again. They left the Chicago Theater in 1839, and it was turned back into an auction house; obviously, a theater was not the best business proposal for a city like Chicago. Chicago went back to its circuses and saloons, forgetting temporarily about its foray into proper comedic theater.

Chicago didn't see another major theater again until 1847, when John B. Rice, a New York transplant, built the Rice Theater. Managing a theater was a full-time job, and Rice, like most theater managers at the time, was an actor, scene painter and anything else that was needed. Apparently, Mr. Rice was a good enough actor to have gotten some attention in New York, which made his move to Chicago all the easier. If he could make it in New York, he could certainly make it anywhere.

Chicagoan's needed entertainment. In 1847, there was a cholera epidemic that killed more than six hundred people. Citizens were desperate for something to take away the pain of the dark city. Rice attempted to grant that wish when he presented Chicago's first opera, *La Sonnumbula*, in 1850. He hoped the opera would bring a large crowd into his theater, but on opening night, the opera was sparsely attended. During the performance, the warning cry of fire broke, and the audience jumped out of their seats, eyes darting to the nearest exit. The ever-present John Rice cried, "Sit down! Sit down! Do you think I would permit a fire to occur in my theater?"[5] For a moment, the audience members stared back at Rice until their senses got the better of them. The fire grew out of control and took over the stage just as the audience made it out. And although not a comedic experience in any way, leave it to the residents of Chicago to provide the greatest comedic relief:

> *Mr. B. and a small party of jolly English friends, who had been dining out, concluded to patronize the opera that evening, and Mr. B., whose rotundity was considerably better filled with the sparkle than the rest, had taken a front seat, and was saluting the song and sentiment of the occasion with unbounded applause, by clapping his hands and vociferating "bravo! bravo!" Presently, like an electric shock, came the cry of "fire!" The audience started suddenly for the doorway, though their retreat was checked to good order by Mr. Rice, who was on the stage at the time. Then all was confusion, and each member of the company, in endeavoring to save the properties, was rushing backward and forward across the stage. Meanwhile our friends outside had missed their comrade, and thinking perhaps he might have been injured, one of them stepped up to the boxes, just as the fire was bursting through the end of the building, in volumes, and Rice was crossing the stage with a side scene on his shoulder. There sat Mr. B., solitary and alone, on the front seat, in perfect ecstasies at the performance, shouting "Bravo! Bravo! the most splendid imitation of a fire I ever saw!"* [6]

The new Rice Theater opened in 1851, designed by the renowned architect John Van Osdel, who would later build a hotel for Potter Palmer, one of the richest men in Chicago. The new theater was done entirely in brick.

One important stock star in Mr. Rice's theater was Mrs. John Drew, the grandmother of Lionel, Ethel and John Barrymore. Also well known in Rice productions was a comedian named James McVicker. McVicker was a traveling comedian looking for a permanent home. After Dan Marble, Rice's stock comedian, passed away, McVicker paid a visit to Marble's widow. He purchased all Marble's costumes, making it quite easy for Rice to replace Marble with McVicker. McVicker became so well known and famous that he eventually left for New York to pursue bigger dreams, a theme Chicago would end up dealing with well into the twenty-first century.

Mr. Rice was also instrumental in bringing the Christy Minstrels to Chicago, one of the first minstrelsy groups to appear in the city. Even though the Rice Theater presented mostly dramatic works, Rice would end the show on a laugh, knowing his Chicago audiences were reluctant to sit through an entire drama. In 1857, John Rice gave up his career in the theater but would not soon give up his career on stage. In 1865, Rice was elected to an entirely different kind of theater when he was named mayor of Chicago. He was mayor from 1865 to 1869, proving that the link between Chicago theater and Chicago politics was a fine line indeed.

3
IF YOU BUILD IT,
THEY WILL COME

If at first, the idea is not absurd, then there is no hope for it.
—*Albert Einstein*

Chicago held on to its frontier town status even though it had been incorporated as a city in 1837. New Yorkers held on tight, hoping against hope that the money and time they had invested would come to fruition, and in 1848, to fruition they came. Louis Jolliet's dream of a canal that would connect the Illinois to the Mississippi became a reality. The Illinois/Michigan Canal was finished in 1848, and now there was a direct waterway from the east to the west. This was an important canal; not only did it connect New York and its goods to the burgeoning West, but it also brought people to the city to work on the canal. Immigrants from all over the world came to the city to find work and live the American dream. Chicago's population jumped from four thousand to a mighty twenty thousand strong in a matter of years. The canal meant that Chicago's place as a transportation hub was now secure. Everything passed through Chicago—lumber, goods, wheat and, most importantly, people. In just one day in 1857, over thirty-four hundred immigrants arrived to Chicago from New York.

Chicago was built by people with crazy ideas. From Jolliet's unused plans for the French to Isherwood and his theater, Chicago didn't happen by men listening to whispering doubts. The city's first mayor, William Butler Ogden, had a crazy idea, too, and he wasn't about to let a little criticism quiet his active brain. Ogden was the first of many mayors to realize that what was good for Chicago was good for him. He was interested in increasing Chicago's reach around the country, and in a move that would change forever not only Chicago, but also Chicago's comedy scene, Ogden laid the first line of railroad track.

No one else agreed that the railroad was the best thing for Chicago. Investors from New York feared that the railroad would prevent farmers from staying in Chicago as they would with a horse and carriage. Instead of counting on money from the easterners and the new elite of Chicago, Ogden went out on his own to the hinterlands of the prairies. The farmers he talked to were extremely interested in a railroad. Ogden sold shares to them and laid the first track in 1848. Ogden's risk paid off; in just a few years, these weblike structures would fan out in all four directions from the city proper. The railroads changed everything. Not only was Chicago doing big business on the waterways, but also the railroad now connected everything to Chicago and Chicago to everything. Other potential cities had maybe one or two exports they called their own, but Chicago exported and imported almost everything.

By 1857, Chicago had the largest railway network in the world. The frontier town of just twenty years earlier was long gone. Now Chicago had fancy hotels, retail stores and even more opportunity to make money. Chicago was moving at such a quick pace that even Mayor Ogden admitted that maybe the city needed to develop "culture, taste, beauty, art, literature, or there was a danger that [it] will become a town of mere traders and money getters; crude, unlettered, sharp and grasping."[1] Chicago was a place where people believed they could come make a quick buck. Culture was not its priority. The city attracted men who wanted to work hard and play hard and make a buck as quickly as possible, no matter the moral ambiguities. It was a "city of strangers, it was a paradise for pickpockets, confidence men, and streetwalkers."[2] Nelson Algren, author of *City on the Make*, said of early Chicagoans:

> *They hustled the land, they hustled the Indian, they hustled by night and they hustled by day. They hustled guns and furs and peltries, grog and the blood-red whiskey-dye; they hustled with dice or a deck or a derringer. And decided the Indians were wasting every good hustler's time...They were out to make a fast buck off whoever was standing nearest.*[3]

Chicago's growth was unparalleled. As immigrants and easterners poured into the city, everyone was on the search for new entertainment. But Chicago wasn't like New York; there was no set way of doing things in Chicago. According to Tim Samuelson:

> *If you were unintentional in your thinking and you didn't fit in to traditional roles, be it business or theater, you were still in an old city or community and there's been enough time to evolve on how things should or shouldn't be done. But all bets are off in Chicago because people came here from all over; there was no consensus on how anything should be done, or how they should perform. People could come here and do their own thing, they could do whatever [they] wanted in Chicago just by the nature that no one was going to tell you not to.*[4]

James McVicker was used to doing his own thing. After buying the costumes of the dead comedian Dan Marble, McVicker went to make it big in New York. But as many others would do, McVicker returned to Chicago to pursue his own dream of opening a theater. McVicker's Theater opened in 1857. It was a much nicer place than the Rialto or the Chicago Theater. McVicker's Theater was described as

> *a pretentious structure for its time, its cost being $85,000. It had a seating capacity for 2,500 people and with its equipment, it was by all odds the best and the most commodious playhouse in the west. Its opening event was the crowning event of the drama in Chicago up to that time. The opening performance was* The Honeymoon *and* Rough Diamond. *In both, Mr. McVicker sustained the comedy element.*[5]

McVicker's was a more wholesome place to go to the theater. Although women were shunned from the shows in nearby saloons, McVicker realized he could get twice the money if he allowed women and children to come to his theater—on designated days of course. McVicker did his best to offer high-class drama but was a good enough businessman to know that he had to offer other kinds of amusements as well. He would throw in a comedy from time to time to keep his rowdy Chicago audiences in line. One of the shows at the McVicker was *The Sultans of Sulu*, a musical comedy that showed the heartaches of being stranded in a new land, a popular theme for the thousands of immigrants streaming into Chicago.

McVicker drew a line separating comedy from drama. Dramatic work was more appropriate for his world-class theater. Those pesky comedy shows were for the down and out, the drunk and disconnected. Chicago sat patiently somewhere between the two, like a dog choosing between two masters. Tim Samuelson put it this way:

> There are stories about Chicago being a tough place to perform, but see, there's an interesting dynamic, it always had an identity problem. Chicago had this freewheeling soul, but part of it still wanted to be taken seriously, so it's kind of this conflict, but naturalness and informality always won out.[6]

To quell the crowds during dramatic performances, McVicker put up the Christy Minstrels at his theater. Minstrelsy was a common form of comedy in the nineteenth century. White men—and after the Civil War, even African Americans—would dress in blackface and entertain audiences with simple, physical jokes and music. In the present day, it's apparent that minstrel shows were racist and antagonistic, but back then they were incredibly popular. It was often the first time that white people had any contact with blacks at all. It was the closest they would get to seeing what life was like for people different from themselves—although a completely blurred vision.

Minstrel shows proved an important link in the evolution of comedy in Chicago. McVicker was putting on his dramatic written work, full of plot lines and script readings. But minstrel shows broke free from traditional theater. They didn't follow plot lines but filled their shows with music, sketches, dancing and comedy. Minstrel performers were travelers and didn't need elaborate stage sets or costumes. They would travel the railroads in and out of Chicago, performing and perfecting bits all across the Midwest. Although most minstrel shows centered on musical comedy, the "stump speech" was a spoken word piece that occurred in the second act. The stump speech was basically a monologue poking fun at the political or social statements of the day. The stump speech was the precursor to what would become modern-day stand-up comedy.

Things moved along nicely in Chicago. Success seemed to be in the air for the city and for the theaters within it. Theaters and businesses were popping up all the time. Piggybacking on the success of McVicker's Theater, Hooley Opera House opened in 1871. Richard M. Hooley arrived in Chicago by way of New York. Although Hooley's father wished that he would pursue a career in the medical field, Hooley came to Chicago to search out his own dream: music and art. He started out with producing minstrel shows, and after seeing the vibrancy and excitement of the shows in New York, he knew he had fallen in with the right business. He moved to Chicago in 1871 and purchased Bryan's Hall on Clark Street. He named his new theater Hooley's Opera House, attracting only the best of Chicago society.

Unfortunately for Hooley, his timing was a little off.

4

GONNA BE A HOT TIME IN THE OLD TOWN TONIGHT

As there has never been such a calamity, so has there never been such a cheerful fortitude in the face of desolation and ruin.[1]
—*Joseph Medill*

Let's face it, Chicago was built in a rather slapdash manner. As its population soared, the city did the best it could to keep up:

> *Outside the central business district almost every building was constructed of wood, while many of the new marble-faced brick buildings downtown had ponderous wooden cornices, long wooden signs on their fronts, and mansard top stories of wood. And all of them had wooden roofs covered with felt, tar, or shingles. Even the roof of Ellis Chesbrough's fortresslike Water Works, Chicago's first line of defense against fire, was made of wood.*[2]

In 1871, Chicago had been through a long drought, and by October 8, there had only been an inch of rain since July. The northwesterly winds blew as a small fire popped up in Mrs. O'Leary's barn just west of the Loop. The rest of the city slept peacefully, secure in the knowledge that a big fire had been quelled the night before. But by the time poor Mr. O'Leary woke from a fretful sleep, his wife was being blamed for burning the city of Chicago to the ground. The fire started in the O'Leary barn and made its way to the river. The river was completely polluted from years of waste from the slaughterhouses, and it lit up and provided its own portage for the fire to cross into the Loop. The fire demolished seventeen thousand buildings before it burned out on Fullerton Avenue. It left over 100,000 people homeless and over 300 dead.

Mrs. O'Leary led a hard life in Chicago in those years after the fire. Even stepping outside her house would invite opinions from her fellow Chicagoans. The press hounded her so badly that she lived as a recluse for the rest of her life. Forty years after the fire, Michael Ahern, a reporter for the *Chicago Republican*, admitted that he and two other reporters made up the story about the cow kicking over the lamp after they found a broken lantern in the shed. The true story of the Chicago fire is lost to the ages, but Chicago did manage to officially release Mrs. O'Leary of any responsibility—in 1997. Quite a relief for her, I'm sure.

On October 11, 1871, the *Chicago Tribune* ran an editorial with a message of hope: "In the midst of calamity without parallel in the world's history, looking upon the ashes of thirty years' accumulations, the people of this once beautiful city have resolved that Chicago Shall Rise Again."[3] And with those words, the remnants of Chicago Before were dumped into the lake to create the landfill for the Chicago of Now. The spirit of improvisation, of moving forward without any clue about what would happen next, took hold of Chicago. Word spread to New York and every little town that would hear it: in Chicago there was work. A whole city was to be rebuilt, and it would require the best and the brightest to do it. Luckily for Chicago and the easterners attached to it, the city was able to push past the darkness of the fire. The city had made its name in business, and its primary ways of making money were still intact. The railroads were still viable, the stockyards were safe and the Illinois/Michigan Canal was still letting in the big boats from all over the world.

Richard Hooley's Opera House burned down in the fire. It changed his whole path. Before the fire, Hooley

> *intended to take the morning train to New York. He intended to retire from the profession of which he had long been an honored member, to enjoy a handsome competency which a life of labor and energy had enabled him to accumulate. Much of his fortune was invested in this city. The fire came and swept away the earnings of thousands, his among the rest. But his spirit was not broken, and with gallant courage he went to work to repair the ravages of the fire. How well he succeeded was apparent last evening to those who visited his beautiful theater on the occasion of its opening.*[4]

Hooley jumped right back in and reopened his theater, and it was even grander than the one before. He called his new theater Hooley's Parlor Home of Comedy. Mr. Hooley became known as one of the great theater managers of all time, bringing a variety of shows to the new fourteen-hundred-seat theater. Hooley's old pal James McVicker was there to see the opening of the new theater and give him a pat on the shoulder for a job well done.

The Chicago fire changed everything about the city. Without it, Chicago would not be the same magnificent city that it is today. Chicago got a second chance. Perhaps that's why it has always been accepting of failure; it is in Chicago's blood to give it another go. And although a greater metropolis was to rise out of the ashes, Mayor Ogden mourned the city he lost:

> *Never before was a large and very beautiful and fortunate City built by [a] generation of people so proud, so in love with their work, never a City so lamented and grieved over as Chicago. For this I do weep with those who have far greater occasion to weep than I.*[5]

Chicago was a serious city. After the fire, William LeBaron Jenney built the first ever skyscraper in 1885, and huge stone buildings crowded the people and the skyline. The people were rebounding from one of the greatest tragedies to occur in any city. Corruption, vice and greed were alive on every corner; hogs and cows were being butchered by the thousands; and pollution, smog and smoke clouded the vision of all who walked through the Loop. Yet, in the midst of it all, Chicago continued to find its sense of humor in the face of tragedy. In his poem "Chicago," the great poet Carl Sandburg sensed the emotion:

> *Under the smoke, dust all over his mouth, laughing with white teeth,*
> *Under the terrible burden of destiny laughing as a young man laughs,*
> *Laughing even as an ignorant fighter laughs who has never lost a battle,*
> *Bragging and laughing that under his wrist is the pulse, and under his ribs*
>   *the heart of the people, Laughing!*
> *Laughing the stormy, husky, brawling laughter of Youth, half-naked,*
>   *sweating, proud to be Hog Butcher, Tool Maker, Stacker of Wheat,*
>   *Player with Railroads and Freight Handler to the Nation.*[6]

As the green grasses of Grant Park gave reprieve from the oppression of the city, so laughter provided respite from the sadness of a city burned. After the Chicago fire, more people than ever came to Chicago to build its new destiny. A new day of comedy and showmanship was about to alight in Chicago, once again changing all in its path.

5

THE PHOENIX

I give you Chicago. It is not London and Harvard. It is not Paris and buttermilk. It is American in every chitling and sparerib. It is alive from snout to tail.
—*H.L. Mencken*

C hange was to come to the dark, polluted and corrupt city of Chicago. Only twenty years after the fire burned 17,000 buildings and the entire business district of the Loop, Chicago hosted the Columbian Exposition, a world's fair that would rival all world's fairs. The White City emerged on the south side, and it changed the way the public and performers would view their art and entertainment. Twenty-six million people visited the more than 250 buildings in the year the exposition was open. Fairgoers saw everything from the brand-new Cracker Jack candy to the Ferris wheel. The World's Fair not only changed the way people saw Chicago, but it also changed the way people saw entertainment. The "midway" was a World's Fair invention, a central location with entertainment on all sides that led to the invention of theme parks like Coney Island and Disneyland. The public became used to consuming entertainment and, most importantly, paying for it. Money could be used to entertain oneself. Now people were not only producing entertainment but also paying for it. Entertainment was becoming business.

The fair also changed how people viewed Chicago. Many local entrepreneurs found it an advantageous time to open all kinds of businesses, from dime store museums to variety clubs. Performers of all kinds poured into the city; musicians and comedians saw the white light of the manufactured city before them, but the fact was, the darker, more polluted city was hustling on as ever, paying no attention to the man behind the curtain.

While Chicago's elite began to the learn the difference between comedy and drama and the class ideals attached to it, African Americans were becoming their own force in reshaping comedy and the city itself. After World War I, the migration from Europe came to a trickle while African Americans came here in multitudes. The *Chicago Defender* was established in 1905 by Robert Sengstacke Abbott and was a strong force in bringing blacks to Chicago from the South. Abbott touted the freedom Chicago offered and ran pictures of housing in Chicago comparing it to housing in the South. The *Defender* would even print names and addresses of churches on the south side so people could find a community when they arrived. Naturally, blacks came to Chicago to find a better life for themselves. Since some even had connections to the south side before arriving, that area of Chicago became the focal point for the black community. But in this city of immigrants, African Americans were even lower on the totem pole than the many immigrants who flocked here in the nineteenth century. Even the stockyards, offering some of the worst working conditions in the city, wouldn't hire African Americans unless there was a strike.

The railroads that had been laid fifty years earlier brought jazz musicians and performers from all over the country to Chicago. The south side was creating its own culture, and in 1905, the Pekin Theater opened. It was a pivotal moment, not only in Chicago, but also in the country as a whole. The Pekin was the first theater in the country that was black owned and the first to feature black performers. Robert Mott, the owner of the Pekin, was a successful gambler from the Levee district. The Levee was the red-light district of Chicago, and Mott one of its most successful inhabitants. He opened a gambling house on South State Street and found himself quite the successful businessman. After running a small variety theater in his gambling house, Mott decided he wanted to open a legitimate black theater. This was virtually unheard of at the time; young black men from the south side were not expected to run a successful and legitimate theater. Plus, the white businessmen had a lot of money invested in their theaters and kept a tight leash on new theaters encroaching on their business.

Once Mott opened the Pekin, many other black theaters followed suit. The Pekin proved that a black-owned theater could be successful. Mott added legitimacy to his theater by presenting full-on dramatic and scripted plays in addition to his variety comedy lineup. The performers worked at a feverish pace, often rehearsing and writing in the morning and performing that same night. Since Mott still had a small audience base, he needed to change shows every two weeks. The amount of work that poured out of that theater in regards to music, drama and comedy was unparalleled for its time.

Many whites at the time couldn't even imagine a black entrepreneur being successful, yet the Pekin was a classy place, and it surprised people. The ticket cost was high, and Mott went to great trouble to make his former gambling den worthy of a costly ticket price. He built box seats, an orchestra pit and a beautiful stage; the costumes, lighting and sets were all of the highest quality. In 1908, *Theater* magazine remarked:

> *No white man's name appears on the payroll in any capacity. The theater is scrupulously clean, neat and tasteful. It seats 900 persons. The house boasts an innovation in the way of a physician, constantly in attendance. As an enterprise, it has been a success.*[1]

Mott's theater was located on the south side "Stroll." The Stroll was the center of the black entertainment district and the birthplace of jazz. During the day, the Stroll was an excellent place to stop and gossip, but at night all the jazz clubs opened, and the Stroll was home to a variety of entertainment. The Pekin encouraged whites to come to its shows; even Ms. Bertha Palmer, the most powerful woman in Chicago, would enjoy shows at the Pekin Theater, breaking down barriers that had been put up some time ago.

Many wondered why Mott chose the name the Pekin, for his theater. Although there is no hard evidence, it's assumed that either Mott chose a name that would not scare away an interracial audience or he wanted to conjure up a far-off place, a theater of escape for the hardworking people of Chicago.

As industry grew in Chicago, however, many rural people began to settle in the city, and they wanted to see more vaudeville-type shows—simple and easy. Chicago was caught in the crossfire again. It tried to please all its inhabitants, and Mott did the same. He held on to the variety shows common to the lower class but tried to intersperse serious drama as well. After Mott opened a theater on the north side, the Pekin started to creep downhill. Mott passed away in 1911, and on his deathbed, he whispered his wish that the Pekin should never be under the control of white owners.

After his death, his sister held on to the theater but eventually sold it to white owners, who ripped out the box seats and the beautiful stage and relegated the Pekin to a down-and-out dance club. But for years after his death, it was supposed that the ghost of Mott walked the theater, forcing the curtain to stick at the most inopportune moments.

6

ON THE ROAD

Men in this city do not mind failures, and when they have failed,
instantly begin again. They make their plans on a large-scale,
and they who come after them fill up what has been wanting at first.
—Anthony Trollope

Chicago moved into a new age, a post-fire age. By 1900, the city had a population of roughly 1.7 million people. The stockyards were humming along, using and abusing their immigrant workers to rake in the cash. The Levee was in full swing, serving the needs of the busted workers from the slaughterhouses. The First Ward, the richest district in the world, held parties in the name of its corrupt, yet helpful, aldermen: Hinky Dink Kenna and Bathhouse John. The parties were anything goes, harkening back to the old days of the Sauganash. There were raucous performances, illicit dances between whites and blacks and cross-dressing performers who would entertain audiences as liquor and votes were exchanged under faint light. The railroads spread out to the suburbs, reaching out farther than any horse and carriage ever could. Chicago was growing at a breakneck speed, and another kind of theater and performer was on the rise.

Bathhouse John Coughlin was an eclectic character. As an alderman in the Levee District, he would walk the area in his pink and purple overcoats. He was a consummate performer who loved to read his poem, "Dear Midnight of Love," at one of the many vaudeville theaters. Modeled after shows seen at places like the Sauganash, the new vaudeville theaters were venues where one could see a music group, a comedian, a minstrel show, a plate spinner or one man who did it all.

No one knows exactly where the word "vaudeville" hails from, but most likely the term came from the French *voix de ville*, or "voice of the city." The term came into popularity in the 1870s, and the first reference to vaudeville in Chicago was seen in an advertisement for "The Faker of Siva." The Faker was a

> *most wonderful Predistigadore and has proved himself superior to all who have appeared, and has created astonishing sensations before the most fashionable crowded houses. The stock dramatic company will provide additional entertainment by presenting favorable vaudeville each night during the stay of the Faker.*[1]

Vaudeville was a direct descendant of the variety and minstrel shows seen in Chicago's bars and dens of iniquity. The term vaudeville was adopted to separate it from the variety and minstrel shows of the lower class. Even the fancy word "vaudeville" seemed foreign and interesting to the middle class, the exact audience vaudeville was aiming for.

Tony Pastor, a circus ringmaster from New York, saw the potential of the new art form rising out of the darkness in cities like Chicago. In his travels, he saw the amazing talent at the variety shows, dime store museums, freak shows and burlesques around the country. Pastor, like McVicker before him, saw his ticket sales doubling if women were allowed in to see the shows. Pastor elevated the form, inspiring "polite vaudeville," a new kind of show where decent language and beautiful theaters were married to comedic performances that had previously been relegated to bars and barns.

Chicago was a perfect place for the emerging form of vaudeville. Railroad lines made it easy for the performers to travel to and from Chicago. Samuelson says:

> *That's because the central location and the rail hub were a performer's lifeblood. Vaudeville performers depended on scheduling a sequence of acts where they could hop on a train and go anywhere. Just like you could manufacture products anywhere now, you could also organize your tour by hopping on and off the train.*[2]

Vaudeville also appealed to a wide variety of people. Common in vaudeville shows were comedies or comedians who incorporated old world jokes into their acts. The skits often centered on being a foreigner in a new place. Immigrants connected with this style of comedy, recognizing their own fears in the laughter. Since vaudeville performers traveled so much, it was common at the time for acts to include each member of the family. Sons and daughters, children of five and six years old, would perform in the grand theaters, right next to their parents, making vaudeville itself a family affair. Women and children were welcome—at designated times, of course. They were able to enjoy the shows considering most had strict guidelines on what language was allowed to be spoken. Stage doors would support signs from theater managers warning, "Don't say 'slob' or 'son of a gun' or 'hully gee' on the stage unless you want to be canceled peremptorily. Do not address anyone in the audience in any manner."[3] This manifesto assured theater owners of a clean show available to all audiences.

Polite vaudeville brought comedy to high society. Before, opera had been the entertainment of the elite; the middle class enjoyed minstrel shows; and the lower class was used to seeing its entertainment in the saloons, garnering wrath from local pastors. But vaudeville shows were held in huge theaters that could seat from seven hundred to one thousand people a pop. The Chicago School of Architects designed theaters fit for kings. Ushers wore white gloves and were trained extensively on how to deal with Chicago's varying elite. Curtains and lavish interiors led people to believe they were seeing a higher level of art. However, once inside, some vaudeville shows were filled with lewd (and racist) jokes, women with barely any clothes on and more hidden liquor than you could imagine. Some theaters ran shows from eleven in the morning until midnight, varying the raciness of the show depending on what time of day it was.

Vaudeville was a huge force in selling comedy as an art form. Most vaudeville shows wouldn't hear of having a dramatic show at their theaters. Owners wanted continuous streams of laughter. Comedy was a high commodity, and everyone wanted a piece of the pie. Vaudeville was cheap and easy to produce; minstrel shows had already proven that there was no need for the fancy sets and costumes inherent to dramatic theater. Performers had little else but their own personalities to sell. The comedy became decidedly more physical in nature. Before the invention of the microphone, stars found that spoken word comedy didn't translate well in the cavernous theaters. Exaggerated physical and vocal comedy won out, and comedy became less about something political and more about making fun of someone else or acts of schadenfreude.

One of the first vaudeville theaters in Chicago was the West Side Museum started by C.E. Kohl and George Middleton in 1882. They both had a history in the circus and leveraged that into building dime store attractions that could stay in one place rather than move around. Dime stores were big businesses in the late nineteenth century, offering everything from beauty contests to freak shows to gum-chewing contests. At first, people were more than willing to pay their dimes to come in, but soon audiences grew leery of giving their dimes for empty promises. In 1900, Kohl bought out Middleton and began working with his theater manager, George Castle. They saw the writing on the wall of the outdated dime store business and began to open beautiful theaters for fancier vaudeville shows. The two built the most successful vaudeville theaters of all time, including the Olympic, the Majestic, the Haymarket, the Academy of Music and the Star. Eventually, they sold out to the Orpheum out of San Francisco, owners of the "big-time" vaudeville theaters. George Middleton explained his consternation about the need for bigger and better shows:

> It is strange that all large things are more attractive to the public than small things. A large horse is more attractive generally than a small one; a large man is more attractive than a small one. I do not know why it is, but it is undoubtedly true in everything except a woman.[4]

One woman who was living large was Minnie Marx. Sam and Minnie Marx had four sons who had been on the vaudeville circuit for a few years out of New York City. Chico, Harpo, Gummo and Zeppo were known as the singing group the Four Nightingales. Minnie knew that Chicago was vaudeville booking heaven, and she moved her four sons to Chicago in 1910. Chicago had a tightknit community of vaudeville performers, and it was an efficient place to come and perfect an act. The city was filled with performers, but it wasn't high stakes like New York City. Comedians could experiment in Chicago—take a little more time and come to their comedy a little more slowly. The Four Nightingales saw that comedy was the new business, and Minnie and the boys started working on a new act. The brothers wrote a comedy show called *Fun in Hi Skule* in 1910. In *The Marx Brothers: A Bio-Bibliography*, author Wes Gehring states:

> Fun in Hi Skule *was an important transition for several reasons. First, the emphasis of the act was now on comedy. And this first use of Peasie Weasie material, a then-popular style of comic song (based upon word plays such as puns) in vaudeville and burlesque, would foreshadow the later non-stop verbal slapstick of the team's mature work.*[5]

Gehring goes on to note that the show also helped develop the later characters of both Groucho and Harpo.

The Marx Brothers were not so much for script or plot. They learned to improvise during their shows, sometimes even wandering out into the audience to give their shows a different feel. Samuelson says:

> *I think the nature of their mature work, and of course that's when they had been in Chicago as young men developing their style, reflects the impact of Chicago as part of what they did. It's not real typical of what the theater would have been like in New York.*[6]

Another gift came to the brothers during their stay in Illinois. In a poker game in Walesburg, monologist Art Fisher teased the brothers with nicknames. Fisher, who was sharing a double bill with the brothers, gave them their famous aliases. Leonard was a notorious ladies' man, or "chick chaser," and so was named Chicko (later Chico). Arthur played the harp and so was called Harpo. Groucho had the most testy, temperamental attitude, hence Groucho. Milton, or Gummo, was named for the thick gumshoes he always wore. It's not clear why Herbert got the nickname Zeppo—a mystery for the ages. After that fateful poker game, the Marx Brothers were born.

The house in the center is the Bucktown home where the Marx Brothers lived during their ten-year stay in Chicago. *Photo courtesy of John Eiberger.*

The family lived in a house in modern-day Bucktown, but after finding so much success in Chicago, Minnie Marx thought it best to get them to the Broadway stage. She moved them back to New York in 1920. Yet Chicago, once in the blood, is always in the blood, and in 1933, the Marx Brothers pressed their hands into the sidewalk at the Hollywood Walk of Fame. After hearing the directions, Groucho quipped, "There was no need to inform us of the protocol involved. We were from Chicago and knew all about cement."

While the Marx Brothers learned the Chicago way of improvisation and a more "natural" style of comedy, another great vaudeville comedian was making his name known. Shelton Brooks was a Canadian by birth and came to Chicago via Detroit in 1905. Like many other performers of his time, Brooks was a vaudeville performer with a variety of acts under his name. Brooks was a black man who gained respect performing his impressions of Bert Williams. Bert Williams was a black comedian running the vaudeville circuit and was the first black man to grace a Broadway stage. Williams once saw Brooks do an impression of him and declared, "If I'm as funny as he is, I got nothing to worry about." Comedy wasn't the only thing Brooks and Williams had in common; both were successful songwriters and musicians as well.

Shelton Brooks made his big comedy debut in 1911 with the premiere of his first musical comedy, *Dr. Herb's Prescription or It Happened In a Dream*. The show premiered at the Pekin Theater and shot Brooks to stardom. He was one of the first to move away from minstrelsy and blackface. He used his own voice as his humor instead of hiding behind a character. Also, Brooks was one of the first black men on Broadway, a road that had already been paved by Bert Williams.

Although Brooks entered the business as a comedian, he was best known as a songwriter. One afternoon, Brooks was walking around with a tune in his head that he just couldn't get rid of. He sat down in a diner and overheard a couple arguing. He heard an angry woman retort, "Some of these days, you're going to miss me honey." Brooks knew immediately that he had heard the words that matched his tune. His song "Some of These Days" was a big hit for one woman in particular. Sophie Tucker loved the song so much that she adopted it as her theme song and even named her autobiography *Some of These Days*. In her autobiography, Tucker writes:

> *The minute I heard "Some of These Days" I could have kicked myself for almost losing it. A song like that. It had everything. Hasn't it proved it? I've been singing it for thirty years, made it my theme song. I've turned it*

inside out, singing it every way imaginable, as a dramatic song, as a novelty number, as a sentimental ballad, and always audiences have loved it and asked for it. "Some of These Days" is one of the great songs that will be remembered and sung for years and years to come.[7]

Brooks lived in a happy time. World War I was over, and Americans celebrated technology and ingenuity. Elaborate Art Deco skyscrapers shot higher into the sky than ever before. People were having "tango teas" (more whiskey than tea) and staying out all night in one of one hundred saloons. One of Brooks's best-known songs was "All Night Long," a song about the clubs most likely run by Hinky Dink and Bathhouse John Coughlin. Brooks went on to write such crowd pleasers as "The Darktown Strutter's Ball" and "Walkin' the Dog." He was one of the first recorded jazz musicians and paved the way with his comedy and his music. By moving away from minstrelsy and using his own natural style, Brooks contributed greatly to the Chicago style.

The transient nature of vaudeville had found a home in the grand theaters of downtown and the neighborhood bars of a fleeting city. Chicago bustled as vaudeville bustled. The artists of vaudeville mirrored the population of Chicago; comedians, songwriters and actors moved from town to town, rarely settling down in one spot. But as Chicago grew older, its cultural roots grew deeper. People settled in the city, built houses and found communities. To some, Chicago was home. It was an easy city to experiment in; it was less expensive than New York, and land and space were readily available.

The vaudeville theaters began to lose customers when their competitors played the fancy new moving pictures. Audiences got polished entertainment for their money now; the days of slapstick comedy were on their way out, and a subtle, quiet and controlled comedy was being ushered in. Moving pictures were the new game, and Chicago provided a lot of freedom to filmmakers. Production costs were lower, and really, no one was paying attention to what was going on in silly little Chicago. That is, until two con men stole the biggest movie star of all time right from under New York's nose.

7

THE MEDIUMS

Chicago is different because it's not on a coast, it's different from New York or Los Angeles because you have the right to fail. You get more than one chance. You have the right to fail and pick yourself up and start again.
—*Bernie Sahlins*

Essanay Studios was located on the north side of Chicago. Originally called Peerless Film Manufacturing Company, the studio opened in 1907 and had its name changed to Essanay Studios. The name Essanay came from the first initials of the owners' last names, *S* and *A*. George Spoor and Gilbert Anderson were the hustlers Nelson Algren warned us about. Classic Chicago hucksters out to make a buck, they saw the popularity of the new art form and opened Essanay to cash in. But the stock stars at the local theaters weren't so sure of this motion picture madness. They didn't consider it on the same level of stage work and weren't interested in the crazy ideas of two naïve filmmakers. So Spoor and Anderson did what so many in Chicago did: they pulled together what they had and made it work.

Ben Turpin was a janitor at Essanay. Lucky for Spoor and Anderson, he was also a vaudeville and circus star known for his crossed eyes. Turpin believed that his crossed eyes, which he received after an accident when he was a kid, were the most promising part of his career. He even went so far as to get an insurance policy should his eyes ever become uncrossed. Later, it was discovered that Turpin's left eye was actually quite normal, and he would purposely cross it to match his right one when he was on screen. Turpin was

Essanay Studios is now home to St. Augustine's College. *Photo courtesy of John Eiberger.*

famous for his pratfalls, his most famous being his "hundred an eight," a takeoff on a 180-degree somersault. Ever paranoid, each time Turpin did his fall, he raced to a mirror to make sure his eyes hadn't uncrossed. Maybe Turpin's most famous legacy is that in the 1909 film *Mr. Flip*, he received what very well might have been the first pie in the face. It's the small victories.

Essanay gained fame for producing the "Broncho Billy" film shorts. Gilbert Anderson was the first real Wild West star, jumping on the horse before Will Rogers or John Wayne. Essanay churned out the films; from 1907 to 1915, Anderson made 375 westerns. Most of these movies were improvised, too. There's not much time to rehearse and write while filming two to five films a week. Anderson was out to make the big bucks. He knew the entertainment business was fleeting, and he had to go for it while he had it. So even though Broncho Billy was a hit as far as Essanay was concerned, a big city needed a big star.

On the sneak, Gilbert Anderson stole Charlie Chaplin from Keystone Studios with an offer of $1,250 a week, plus a bonus of $10,000—a nice amount of cash. Yet Anderson never told his partner about all the money he was giving to Chaplin, and Spoor wasn't so pleased. The first film they made together was *My New Job*, a parody of Chaplin's former employer. The film was a success, but the working relationships were less than to be desired. Chaplin made over fourteen movies at Essanay, often using the cross-eyed Turpin as his sidekick. The two didn't work so well together, however. They were practicing two different forms of comedy. Chaplin was learning to be subtle and methodical in his comedy, but Turpin came from slapstick and vaudeville. Spoor and Anderson gave Chaplin plenty of freedom and the production requirements to make the types of movies he wanted to make. In Chicago, Chaplin had the freedom to experiment with a more mature style of comedy.

Chaplin became amazingly famous. His improvisation skills were unparalleled, and he was a comedian like no one had ever seen. Other studios noticed what Essanay had and started sniffing around. Chaplin wasn't a big fan of Chicago or Essanay; he hated the cold, and he didn't like the way Spoor and Anderson were running the company. Spoor and Anderson were fighting. Sometimes punches were pulled, and Chaplin was finished. Spoor pulled out a pocket of nasty tricks to try and get Chaplin to stay. He even went so far as blackmailing Chaplin by threatening to publish pictures in the *Chicago Tribune* of Chaplin's mother, who was incredibly sick with syphilis and lived in a sanatorium. Chaplin left Essanay in 1915. Turpin most likely saw the demise of Essanay and left too. After talking pictures were invented, Turpin retired from the film world, occasionally making appearances to get a few laughs. When Turpin passed away in 1940, many people sent flowers, but the largest arrangement, a seven-foot-high display, was from none other than Charlie Chaplin.

Essanay closed its doors only ten years after it opened. Economically, Chicago was a wonderful place to produce film; aesthetically, maybe not so much. The cold drove Chaplin away, and it drove away the film industry as well. Film needs light and cooperation, and the darkness of Chicago was just too insistent. Hollywood was all light, all the time—a perfect place to call home for the film industry. But Chicago wasn't even close to finished. There was another medium that cared not for light, snow, rain or appearance. Radio was a turning point for a comedian wanting to express himself and a new way for the Chicago style of comedy to make an impact on the world.

New York busied itself with theater, Los Angeles immersed itself in film and Chicago, which had money for neither, became a playground for radio. Tim Samuelson says:

> *Any media is something that evolves, and in the case of radio it evolved from stage performances. Initially you have people on air speaking in theatrical voices. You had to speak over static-filled radio, so it was common*

to have dramatic pauses and a booming voice. But for Chicago it was very conversational, it wasn't stage-like. There was a transition between theater and the elocution-lecture style into a more conversational style. It was different and refreshing.[1]

Since no one of any great importance was looking over Chicago's shoulder, experiments were tried and sometimes failed. But the freedom led the comedians and stars of radio to realize that the listener was as close to the radio as the mic was to the performer. It was this natural style of conversation that led to some of the greatest radio shows of all time.

Vaudeville performers did their best to transition into the radio business. But it wasn't always an easy move, as comedians who had relied on their faces—men like Ben Turpin—now had to rely on their voices. The other challenge of radio was that vaudeville actors were always traveling. Since they were always playing a new town, they could do their bits over and over, and they never got stale. With the radio, the same listeners would tune in every week and expect new content. Vaudeville was a perfect stage for a well-performed and well-timed joke, but radio required quick, improvisational bits that could be changed at a moment's notice. Radio was less about gags and more about the humor that comes from characters and relationships.

James Jordan and Marian Driscoll were a real-life couple who traveled the vaudeville circuit together. Born in Peoria, the two made it to Chicago in 1924. Even though they perfected their act on the stage, the two found their true voices on the radio. After playing with a variety of formats, including *Luke and Mirandy* in 1927 and *The Smith Family*, the two started *Smackout* in 1931. *Smackout* was a fifteen-minute radio show about a store owner, Luke Grey, and the various characters who shopped in his store. The titular bit came from the owner always being "smack out" of whatever customers were looking for.

In 1936, Jordan and Driscoll debuted *Fibber McGee and Molly* on WMAQ in Chicago. It struck an immediate chord with the American public. The Depression hit hard, and the married characters of *Fibber McGee and Molly* were having as hard a time as anyone. But they were always hopeful and upbeat. The listening audience could tune in and commiserate. Originally, the show started as a musical variety show, but the actors and the sponsor worked hard on the show—working on timing, pacing and character until eventually it turned into one of the first real situational comedies. The same characters would return week after week, and audiences would tune in to hear their favorite characters, like Old Timer, a hard-of-hearing senior who constantly called Fibber "Johnny" and referred to Molly as "Daughter." The show also made good use of the "running gag," a bit it would use again and again that (hopefully) got funnier each time. Their most famous running gag was "the Closet." Fibber always had too many things in his closet, and every time he opened it, the sound of a million things falling out would make the audience laugh.

Fibber McGee and Molly played with the form of situational comedy, but two other vaudeville comedians went back to an older form of comedy to find their voices. Freeman Gosden and Charles Correll were two white men who had been performing minstrelsy and vaudeville since they were children. They met each other in South Carolina, where they performed together on the vaudeville stages as musicians and comedians.

The two men started their radio careers as *Sam and Henry*, originally broadcast on WGN in 1926. The show was a success, and Gosden and Correll wanted to put recordings of their shows on phonograph records and hand them out to other radio stations. WGN declined because it was fearful of losing control of one of its hottest commodities. But in declining, it did just that. Gosden and Correll left WGN and went to WMAQ, which let

Freeman Gosden and Charles Correll sign books for their fans. *Photo courtesy of the Chicago History Museum.*

them distribute their records to radio stations outside of its range, essentially setting up the first syndicated radio shows. Since WGN still had the rights to *Sam and Henry*, Gosden and Correll renamed themselves *Amos 'n' Andy*, two transplants from Atlanta making their way in the big city. In 1929, *Amos 'n' Andy* debuted on WMAQ.

Freeman Gosden was the voice of kindhearted, gentle Amos, and Charles Correll was the voice of lazy, devilish Andy. To us today, it appears that *Amos 'n' Andy* was an incredibly racist endeavor. But at the time, it was one of the most popular shows, if not *the* most popular show, on radio. The program aired at 11:00 p.m. and became an instant hit. NBC was so happy, it moved the show to 7:00 p.m. for a more mainstream audience, but there was a huge outcry from the West Coast because its residents were forced to listen in the middle of the workday. NBC listened and, for the first time in history, broadcast the show twice. People stopped everything they were doing to listen to *Amos 'n' Andy*. Movie theaters preempted their regular programming so that everyone could get their fix before the movie started. The estimated audience for *Amos 'n' Andy* was forty million people, of all colors, ages and types. There were even babies named after the two characters. The show was also one of the first franchises, with all kinds of merchandise, like candy bars and film shorts.

Gosden and Correll, like Chaplin, were serious about their comedy. Scripts were written quickly and often not finished until just before airtime. They would do their show with no rehearsals, counting on some of that Chicago improvisation to spruce up their bits. Gosden and Correll didn't sit with each other or look at each other while in the studio, partly to keep in character but more so they didn't break on air—a cardinal sin in comedy. In *On the Air: The Encyclopedia of Old Time Radio*, author John Dunning writes:

> *They never looked at each other during the broadcast—the chance of breaking into laughter was too great. Once Gosden had to douse himself with a glass of water to keep from breaking on the air. They did the show cold, with no rehearsal, believing in the spontaneity this gave them. They were so engrossed in the ten minute sketches they created that, according to announcer Bill Hay, they often left the studios with tears in their eyes.*[2]

Amos 'n' Andy made the difficult move to television in 1951. The problems for the show continued, however. Even though it hired black actors, which was pretty forward thinking for the time, the truth was, it was still two white men calling the shots. The characters were old-fashioned stereotypes of lazy men and mean women. The TV show ended in 1953. In 1964, the station announced it was bringing it back, but by this time, the show was met with wild protest, and by 1966, it was quietly taken off the air. The radio show continued in various forms until 1960.

Certainly there was no doubt that *Amos 'n' Andy* was one of the most beloved radio shows of all time, but it is curious how such an offensive show could garner so much popularity. Gosden and Correll helped by making sure they didn't play with politics on *Amos 'n' Andy*. They portrayed southerners as men who always felt the strong pull of home, but this was during the great migration, when blacks were fleeing to Chicago looking for better lives. *Amos 'n' Andy* conveniently never talked about that.

But Gosden and Correll also helped usher in the Chicago School of Radio, and its influence was felt all over the country. Elizabeth McLeod, broadcast historian, notes:

> *As a result of its extraordinary popularity,* Amos 'n' Andy *profoundly influenced the development of dramatic radio. Working alone in a small studio, Correll and Gosden created an intimate, understated acting style that differed sharply from the broad manner of stage actors—a technique requiring careful modulation of the voice, especially in the portrayal of multiple characters. Listeners could easily imagine that that they were actually in the taxicab office, listening in on the conversation of close friends. The result was a uniquely absorbing experience for listeners who in radio's short history had never heard anything quite like* Amos 'n' Andy.[3]

In the 1930s, Chicago was producing over four hundred radio shows, both dramas and comedies like *Amos 'n' Andy*. But as New York and Los Angeles started to heat up and attract more money, many of Chicago's more stalwart stars were lured away. It's the endless story of Chicago. As the other two cities grew, Chicago would constantly fight to keep its talent here. According to Tim Samuelson:

> *Often people would go to New York or Los Angeles, but that wasn't a problem because the whole thing that makes Chicago work is the people coming and going. That person leaves the echo of what they did...and new people are here to try something else. As long as that keeps happening, it's always vital. If it doesn't happen then Chicago could evolve into a place of tradition and lose its oomph.[4]*

The Chicago School of Comedy made another leap with the introduction of television. Although New York was considered the trailblazer in television broadcasting, once again Chicago showed its true colors. A golden age of Chicago comedy was about to make itself known, and the natural style of Chicago continued to produce work that was entirely different from what was going on in the rest of the country.

Burr Tillstrom was always a puppeteer. Born in 1917, Tillstrom grew up in Rogers Park in the North End of Chicago. As a boy, Tillstrom often played with dolls and toys to see how he could manipulate them. One story recalls a time when Tillstrom was sick and stuck in the house, and he ended up giving a show for the kids outside using his windowsill as a puppet booth. He attended the University of Chicago to study drama but eventually left school to show his puppets at the Century of Progress World's Fair held in 1933. He perfected his puppets at vaudeville shows and world's fairs but found a home at the Works Progress Administration (WPA), where he created a puppet for a friend. Tillstrom couldn't bear to part with the puppet and kept him, but he never could find the right name. When Tillman met Tamara Toumanova, a Russian ballerina, she saw the puppet and called him Kukla, the Russian word for doll.

Burr Tillstrom kept Kukla close and traveled with him all over the country. He turned down a trip to Europe when he was asked to be the manager of puppet exhibits at the Marshall Field store in Chicago. The day after his decision to stay in Chicago, Tillstrom saw his first television show and decided that television was the medium for him.

In 1947, Tillstrom brought his puppets Kukla and Ollie to WBKB, Chicago's first television station. At this point, television was something watched at a saloon or someplace outside the house, and the networks wanted something more family oriented. They wanted families to watch television together, at home. Kukla and Ollie, with the addition of Fran Bailey, created a show that parents loved as much as their children. Improvisation once again proved itself to be a driving force behind Chicago's comedy. Tillstrom played all the characters on the show, sometimes switching between voices with nary a moment in between. Fran had a rough idea of what they wanted to talk about that day, but when they went live, she improvised every show. Fran Bailey and Tillstrom were brilliant together. Bailey was a strong asset to the group, able to go with the flow and believe in the puppets and their characters. Much of the joy of *Kukla, Fran and Ollie* was that Bailey believed in the puppets and their characters, and she committed to it. There were very few laugh-out-

Kukla, Ollie, Fran Bailey and Burr Tillstrom smile for the camera. *Photo courtesy of the Chicago History Museum.*

loud moments on the show, but most of the humor stemmed from the relationships between Bailey and the puppets. Kukla and Ollie were not caricatures but full-on personalities, with needs and wants and loves and hates. Part of the joy of the characters is that they learned more about each other as the show went on, as Fran gently prodded and practiced a slower pace of comedy with a big payoff.

Some of what the Chicago style of comedy is, in both television and radio, comes down to money. The radio stations didn't have money for expensive technology and props. Because Chicago didn't have the high budgets that other cities had, it learned to make do with what it had close by. When television came to Chicago, producers did away with fancy cameras and elaborate equipment, even doing away with a studio audience as well. The lack of studio audience meant that the actors could move freely about the stage and use the entire stage to their advantage. This lack of money only solidified the natural style that Chicago was becoming known for. It also led to more experimentation. NBC's station manager at the time said, "New York thinks there's nothing wrong with TV that the stage can't cure, and Hollywood thinks there's nothing wrong with TV that movies can't cure. Chicago goes its own way."[5]

Burr Tillstrom was an influence on another man who epitomized the Chicago style: Dave Garroway. Tillstrom was a regular consultant for the TV show *Garroway at Large* and no doubt influenced the improvisational style for which Garroway would become known. Garroway took up where radio left off and channeled that unpretentious method to television. New York was still trying to make its television studios look like theaters, separating the audience from the actor and engaging a theater stage set. Garroway did away with the audience altogether and talked directly into the camera, giving the impression that he was talking directly to his audience instead of performing a theater piece. Although Garroway was a comedian, he was also an intellectual man with a quiet, relaxed style that led his audiences to trust him implicitly. Garroway, like the radio personalities before him, realized the intimacy of his medium, even though he talked with what seemed like no one listening. *Time* magazine, in an article about Garroway, stated:

> *The Chicago group's imaginative approach has been born of necessity. Lacking big budgets, elaborate equipment and big-name talent, they are forced to shortcut the elaborate. They specialize in what they call "simplified realism" and "ad-lib" drama. By banning studio audiences they can use the four walls of every set; short on cameras, booms and overhead trolleys, they never switch from one camera to another without good reason.*[6]

Improvisation was integral to the Garroway show. Like Tillstrom, Garroway headed out with only a rough outline; the rest of the show would be what it was. Garroway would break the fourth wall by wandering to different parts of the set that were set up to look like completely different sets, essentially showing the viewing audience at home that it was all the trickery of film. Almost as if going through revolving doors, Garroway would introduce multiple characters and interact with each of them. This was a thoughtful way of making his show seem larger than it was, all with less money.

The last *Garroway at Large* aired in 1951. Once again, New York took away one of the city's pioneers. NBC aired the first *Today Show* in 1952, with Dave Garroway as the host, forever imprinting daytime talk shows with the Chicago style of comedy. His natural style and quick wit were a success. He was someone who was easy for the at-home audience to watch, but he was also able to deliver the news in a serious and understandable manner. His nickname was "the Communicator" for his ability to get his point across. Garroway left the *Today Show* in 1961 and appeared here and there, but he never gained the popularity that he once had. Garroway's story ends on a sad note, as so many comedians' stories do. In 1982, Garroway put an end to his own life. His legacy, however, carries over to the histories of so many comedians who followed him. Garroway was essential in creating what would be a warm nest of improvisation for the others who came after him.

A contemporary of Dave Galloway, Studs Terkel was one of Chicago's greatest personalities. Born in 1912, Studs moved to Chicago from New York City when he was ten. He ended up living in Chicago most of his life. He graduated from the University of Chicago Law School in 1934. But Studs never became a practicing attorney and instead joined the Federal Writer's Program for the Works Progress Administration. He did radio announcements and voices for various soap operas. Soap operas were big work in Chicago; the first one broadcast from WGN in 1930.

Terkel was best known for his own radio show *The Studs Terkel Program*, which ran from 1952 to 1957. Terkel was famous for his interviews and histories of common people. As a child, Terkel's parents ran a rooming house. He credited this for his understanding of the common American. He also spent a lot of time at Bughouse Square, a park in Chicago where, every week, people would literally stand on their "soapboxes" and lecture on whatever mattered to them.

Terkel found his way into television with the introduction of *Studs's Place* in 1949. The show was set in a bar with Studs as the bartender. Rich Samuels says, "Imagine *Studs's Place* as *Cheers*—without alcohol (for most of its run), without a laugh track and without a script (the cast improvised on an outline; there was no written dialogue)."[7] Studs, like Garroway and Tillstrom before him, also had no script for his show. *Studs's Place* followed the situational comedy path and portrayed the daily grinds and laughs of a Chicago diner. In a sign of things to come, *Studs's Place* only ran from 1949 to 1950 because the network thought Studs might be a communist. Times they were a-changin', and the comedians of Chicago were about to change with them.

Both Garroway and Terkel were instrumental in creating the Chicago School of Television. Relying on improvisation; small, budgeted sets; and having to use props and sets in the most inventive way they knew how, Chicago television had real character that was completely different from that of New York or Los Angeles. Yet by the 1950s, Chicago's influence in television was starting to wane. With losing its talent to New York and the possibility of coast-to-coast broadcasting, there wasn't much need for broadcasting to come right out of Chicago. But as Fred Allen, a contemporary of Terkel and Garroway, said, "The Chicago shows are making an effort to do something. They're short on money, short on talent, but long on inventiveness."[8]

There were a few comedians who were getting famous on radio and TV, but the majority of stand-up comics were working the same old traveling circuit, playing the bars and saloons that originally called comedy home. Vaudeville helped solidify stand-up as its own art, separate from a general variety-type performer. The public noticed, and stand-up comedy was on the rise. Chicago was a likely place for the stand-up comedian considering all the vaudeville performers who were making their way through the city already. But it also gave rise to comedians who were from Chicago, or at least Waukegan, part of the Chicagoland area.

8

THE SICKNESS

I stay here because there's no other place where I can do what I do, there's no other place to see what I see. I get to see a lot of cool shit.
—*Don Hall*

Jack Benny was born in Chicago as Benjamin Kubelsky in 1848. He grew up in Waukegan, and much to his parents' pride, began to play the violin at the tender age of six. His parents were so proud. Little did they know that their son would become famous for playing the violin, but not in the way they expected. Benny was a terrible student and was expelled from high school. He didn't fare too well in business school either. Benny instead tried his hand at vaudeville; he was much better at comedy than he was at business.

In 1911, Benny was playing the same theater as the Marx Brothers and made a friend in Zeppo Marx. Minnie Marx offered to take the young Benny with them on the road, but Benny's parents wouldn't allow it. Still, the friendship between Benny and Zeppo would last a lifetime. Benny left the stage for a while to enter the navy in 1917. There he learned to entertain the troops with his violin—sort of. One night, when Benny was booed while playing his violin, he improvised his way around it and had the troops laughing. Benny was becoming a comedian as much as he was a musician. From then on, the violin stayed but was mostly used as a comedy prop.

Benny's visit to the *Ed Sullivan Show* in 1932 propelled him to a larger audience and prompted him to start his own radio show. *The Jack Benny Show* premiered in 1932. Benny epitomized what was becoming known as the Chicago style. His stand-up character didn't resemble the real Benny in the least. Benny's character was cheap and vain, had a hard time playing his own violin and insisted he was no older than thirty-nine. This required a lot of confidence on the part of the real Benny. Playing an unlikeable character is not an easy thing to do, but Benny did it with aplomb, allowing his supporting cast to get laughs at his expense. Benny knew this was for the greater good of the show. Several times, Benny was known to say, "I don't care *who* gets the laughs on my show, as long as the *show* is funny." The group mind that Chicago was becoming known for was on its way.

Benny's show was funny; so funny, in fact, that it's rumored he got the longest laugh in radio history. Benny set up the joke by saying he was walking down the street with Ronald Coleman's Oscar statue when he got held up. The mugger asked for a match and then said, "Don't make a move, this is a stickup. Now, come on. Your money or your life." Benny stopped for a moment; the audience laughed, knowing the character that Benny typically played; and then the mugger repeated his demand, "Look, bud! I said your money or your life!" And without a moment's hesitation, Benny said, "I'm thinking it over!" Possibly the greatest punch line of all time.

Benny grabbed at the brass ring of television, and in 1950 *The Jack Benny Show* premiered on TV. Benny's move to television was seamless; his deadpan expression and controlled gestures just made him funnier. He added more sight gags and more interviews, losing some of the characters that were so well known on the radio. In the 1960s, Benny was taken off the television due to the new demographic of young "kids." Benny later said of television, "By my second year in television, I saw that the camera was a man-eating monster. It gave a performer close-up exposure that, week after week, threatened his existence as an interesting entertainer."[1] Benny continued to make movies and worked as a stand-up comedian until his death in 1974.

During the time Benny was honing his skills in the nightclubs of Chicago, it would not be surprising—or maybe it would be—if he saw a young man walking around in an old elephant's cape. Richard Buckley was the proud owner of the cape, which he found in the dregs of a bankrupt circus. He wrapped the cape around his shoulders, declared himself a lord and started performing at speakeasies throughout Chicago. While performing at a mob-owned speakeasy called Suzy Q, Buckley used to ride around town in a hearse. Lord Buckley would put on his best tux and lie down in the back of the hearse. When it pulled up next to an unsuspecting driver, Buckley would sit straight up out of the coffin holding a sign that read: "The Body Comes Alive at the Suzy Q."

Al Capone thought Buckley was hilarious and noted that Buckley "was the only man who could make me laugh." Capone set Buckley up with his own club in Chicago called the Chez Buckley. The lord would host some of the greatest jazz musicians, possibly igniting his love for the black dialect he would use in his comedy in later years. Lord Buckley would point to hypocrisy as he draped himself in royal cloaks but spoke with an unaffected black dialect. According to Barry Sanders, professor emeritus at Pitzer College, Buckley was the "Pied Piper of the Impossible." Sanders continued:

> If we can trace the idea of the interlocutor back to the 19th century in this country, and to minstrelsy and its Jim Crowe routines of white men performing their slaphappy dances in black-face, Buckley crashed the party. He put an end to burnt cork and ushered on to the stage the era of courageous stand-up.[2]

Buckley was the first of the real beat comics. He saw the revolution around the corner. Buckley talked about drugs and jazz and sex. He was cool, and the status quo was uncool. Comedy was becoming a tool of the underground and the political. Stand-up comedy wasn't just set up

Above the former Annoyance Theater, the sign reads "no and." *Photo courtesy of Ken Manthey.*

and punch line anymore; now, stand-up comedy had something to say. Eventually, things got a little too hot for Buckley, and he was forced to leave town under pressure from the vice squad.

Although this book is a history of Chicago comedy and Lenny Bruce wasn't from Chicago, he was a major influence on every comic who followed him. It is almost impossible to document the history of Chicago stand-up without talking about Lenny Bruce. If Lord Buckley made stand-up courageous, then Lenny Bruce "yes anded" that and ushered in stand-up for a new age. Because of Bruce, stand-up became smart, political and truthful. Bruce said the things no one else would say. In the 1950s, an era of McCarthyism and witch hunts, Lenny Bruce brought forth the real "truth in comedy." Lord Buckley started the job of breaking down the walls, cementing the fact that the days of blackface and the simpler days of slapstick were over. But Bruce was the ringleader in a period of philosophical, politically minded, satirical and smart comedy.

Bruce was labeled a "sick comic" by *Time* magazine. In a 1959 article titled "The Sickniks," *Time* explained itself:

> *What the sickniks dispense is partly social criticism liberally laced with cyanide, partly a Charles Addams kind of jolly ghoulishness, and partly a personal and highly disturbing hostility toward all the world. No one's flesh crawled when Jack Benny carried on a running gag about a bear named Carmichael that he kept in the cellar and that had eaten the gasman when he came to read the meter. The novelty and jolt of the sickniks is that their gags ("I hit one of those things in the street—what do you call it, a kid?") come so close to real horror and brutality that audiences wince even as they laugh.*[3]

The words Bruce was speaking in the name of comedy were offensive to some. The sick comics were fighting for First Amendment rights and freedom of speech. During this age of McCarthyism, words carried a lot of weight. People were turned in for a lot less. Bruce's words were enough to get him in serious trouble. He was arrested in 1961 in San Francisco; a year later, he was arrested in Chicago at the Gate of Horn, one of the premier houses for folk music. The judges believed

> *the entire performance was originally held by us to be characterized by its continual reference, by words and acts, to sexual intercourse or sexual organs in terms which ordinary adult individuals find thoroughly disgusting*

and revolting as well as patently offensive; that, as is evident from these brief summaries, it went beyond customary limits of candor, a fact which becomes even more apparent when the entire monologue is considered.[4]

In 1963, Bruce was arrested for drug possession while he was on recess from the Chicago trial. Poor guy couldn't catch a break. The Chicago jury tried him in absentia, and he was sentenced to a year in jail. Bruce remained free on bond until the sentence was reversed in 1964. In Bruce's own words:

One of the things that I got arrested for in Chicago was showing a picture of a girl who was really pretty. I wanted to point out the God-made-the-body paradox of the decent people who would object to that groovy-looking chick.[5]

Bruce was arrested again in Greenwich Village in 1964 and was indicted on an obscenity charge. This was major. Many people came forward pleading his case, arguing that his comedy was social commentary, not just obscenity. But by a vote of two to one, Bruce was sentenced again, this time for four months. Bruce never bounced back after his string of arrests and was found dead in his home from a morphine overdose in 1966. He may have died young—too young—but his legacy produced some of the greatest comedic minds in history. Everything changed after Bruce. Chicago comedy became of the mind, of politics and of intelligence.

Lenny Bruce had his own influences, one of whom was Mort Sahl, the original "sick comic." Sahl was a good friend of Hugh Hefner's and spent a lot of time perfecting his act at the Playboy Club in Chicago. Sahl had a theatrical background, and his stand-up reflected that. Instead of standing on stage with a microphone telling knock-knock jokes, Sahl would stand on stage with a newspaper and riff off the news. He would say things no one could imagine even talking about—mainly concerning segregation, sex and politics. They said it couldn't be done, but Mort Sahl did it. Sahl didn't write jokes like a classic stand-up; rather, he improvised most of his act. But he had a complicated relationship with improvisation:

I become impatient with it and want to start with something else, because every word I do is improvised. I don't rehearse anything. I start it on the stage. I never stress that word: "improvise"; it's become distasteful to me because it's been dissipated by people who don't. People say, "We improvise! We improvise!" Well, I have to. I've found no other way out. That's the easiest way.[6]

Sahl's theatricality, improvisation techniques and political satire influenced more comics than just Lenny Bruce.

Shelley Berman was born in Chicago in 1925. A classically trained actor, Berman was trained at the Goodman Theater and did stock theater in and around Chicago and New York. He hooked up with the Compass Players in the 1950s. The Compass Players were the precursor to what would later become Second City. Although Berman may not have been the best when it came to the idea of "group mind" that the Compass was exploring, he did have the chance to experiment and create his comedy routine there. The telephone bit that Berman perfected in his stand-up was born out of improvisation:

> *I was doing this scene at The Compass, and the phone conversation was getting more involved every night. It got to be a little better and a little longer, and one night, when I finished the phone conversation, the audience applauded as I hung up. So I stopped right there. And that became my first actual telephone monologue.*[7]

The problem was, Berman wasn't so great at playing in an ensemble. Stand-up was calling.

After watching Mort Sahl at a local club called Mister Kelleys, Berman was excited to see that he didn't have to do the classic set up/punch line type of jokes common at the time. He could use his improvisational, theatrical telephone conversations to break into stand-up comedy. Lenny Bruce influenced Mort Sahl, and Sahl was instrumental in shaping Berman. The fact that Berman was so fluent in improvisation was also key to his act. It made him different from other comedians, who would just write out a joke. Even Sahl and Bruce would riff off a particular rant or string a series of words together, but Berman found his comedy through character work. Improvisation became intermingled with carefully chosen words and intellectual pursuits. Berman's bits were a hit. His comedy record, *Inside Shelley Berman*, was released in 1959 and was the first comedy record to go gold. It was also the first nonmusical record to receive a Grammy. Berman was also the first comedian to ever play Carnegie Hall.

Berman still performs. He was most recently seen playing Larry David's father on *Curb Your Enthusiasm*. In an interview with *Shecky* magazine on January 18, 2000, *Shecky* asks Berman which were his favorite clubs to play— New York, Los Angeles or Chicago. Berman answers, "All three rooms were great to work in. Each had its own kind of inner and outer atmosphere. It is impossible for me to say which was my favorite. But, let's face it, I'm a Chicago boy."[8]

The Annoyance clown from Co-Ed is about as sick and scary as it gets. *Photo courtesy of Ken Manthey.*

The era in which these guys were speaking these unspeakable truths was such a tense and dangerous time. The simpler days of vaudeville seemed light years away. Stand-up was officially an art form with responsibilities. It was no longer smushed between various musical acts; stand-up comedy in Chicago was its own fury. Lord Buckley, Lenny Bruce and Mort Sahl heralded a new day. Now that stand-up comedy was a political force, other comics could come out and say what they thought. And other comics like Dick Gregory took it even one step further.

Dick Gregory was born in 1932 in St. Louis. He won a track scholarship to Southern Illinois University but was drafted into the army after two years. In the army, he performed in a few talent shows and began his stand-up career making fellow soldiers laugh. He moved to Chicago in the late 1950s and started performing comedy at black clubs on the south side. In 1961, while working at the black-owned Roberts Show Bar, Hugh Hefner walked in to check out the scene. Here's a snippet of what Hef heard:

> *Good evening ladies and gentlemen. I understand there are a good many Southerners in the room tonight. I know the South very well. I spent twenty years there one night.*

Last time I was down South I walked into this restaurant and this white waitress came up to me and said, "We don't serve colored people here." I said, "That's all right. I don't eat colored people. Bring me a whole fried chicken." [9]

Gregory said of his stint at the Playboy Club, "It was the first time they had seen a black comic who was not bucking his eyes, wasn't dancing and singing and telling mother-in-law jokes, just talking about what I read in the newspaper."[10] Lord Buckley would have been proud.

After his performance, the Playboy Club extended Gregory's contract from three weeks to three years, and by 1962, Gregory was a well-known name nationwide. He became part of a local scene of other black comics who weren't practicing minstrelsy but actual stand-up comedy. Gregory was one of the first to break the mold of black comics playing only black clubs. He paved the way for the likes of Bill Cosby and Richard Pryor. Gregory's comedy was satirical, ironic and political, just the kind of thing that got under Mayor Daley's skin. And Gregory knew it.

As Dick Gregory's career progressed, his stand-up comedy evolved into a serious interest in politics. His rebellious and activist streak hit a zenith in 1967, when he ran against Daley in the mayoral campaign. In his autobiography *Callus on My Soul*, Gregory writes, "Richard Daley was the current mayor and he was holding the city hostage with fear. We called him 'Master Daley' and I thought it would be nice to take his job."[11] Gregory's reasons for running for mayor mirrored the reason for his comedy. He wanted to point out the hypocrisy and fear, to bring it into the open so it would lose its power. People believed in Gregory, too. When Muhammad Ali finished his heavyweight fight in 1967, he walked right up to the mic and yelled, "Dick Gregory for mayor!" Gregory didn't stop at mayor either. In 1968, he ran for president as a write-in candidate and received over forty-seven thousand votes. Gregory moved to Massachusetts in 1973 and is still active in politics, speaking all over the country about politics and his other passion: veganism.

Another comic who embodied the sick comic side of Chicago comedy, but in a totally different way, was Bob Newhart. Born and raised in Oak Park, Newhart was drafted into the Korean War, and after being discharged in 1954, he came back to Chicago and started work as an accountant. When an accountant's motto is "close enough," it's a surefire sign he's in the wrong business. Newhart knew that being an accountant wasn't his line of work, and he got a job as a copywriter for Fred Niles, a film producer in Chicago. Newhart would tape funny bits with his co-workers and send them to radio stations as an audition. A disc jockey friend finally introduced him to the head of Warner Brothers, and Warner Brothers signed him in 1959, just a year after it opened. Without the same stage time under his belt as a lot of other comics, Newhart recorded his comedy album *The Button-Down Mind of Bob Newhart. Button-Down Mind* is still one of the best-selling twenty albums of all time. He was the first comedy artist to make it on the Billboard charts, stammering right past Elvis's swagger to get there.

Newhart's shtick was completely different from those of other comics. Other comics like Shelley Berman were running around being the funny man. Not Newhart. His thing was that he was the first solo straight man. Keeping a stoic face and voice, Newhart would show that the funny was what was being said on the other line. In his bit *Driving Instructor*, Newhart plays the straight man to an invisible woman on the other line. Although the audience never hears the other person, we can tell from Newhart's deadpan reactions that it is she who is obviously crazy. Newhart's humor came from recognition. His everyman personality appealed to many, and his stammer endeared him to all. Newhart knew the power of his stammer:

> *When I was doing* The Bob Newhart Show, *one of the producers pulled me aside and said that the shows were running a little long. He wondered if I could cut down the time of my speeches by reducing my stammering. "No, that stammer bought me a house in Beverly Hills."*[12]

Newhart also differentiated himself from the other sick comics by being a clean one. Newhart didn't swear and he didn't say obscene words, but he still talked about the things most people wouldn't. His sweet face, kind demeanor and endearing stammer made him a safer comedian.

Newhart was a true Chicagoan. In his memoir, he writes. "It's a city where you say what you mean, mean what you say, and most importantly, where you must be able to back up what you say. All in all, this makes it a great place for a comedian to sharpen their acts."[13] Newhart made Chicago famous in the opening scene of *The Bob Newhart Show*, which ran from 1972 to 1978. Newhart is seen walking across a bridge in Chicago, yet that's not Bob Newhart. His daughter was sick that day, and Newhart called in to say he wouldn't be able to make it to the shoot. The producers were desperate for the shot. They found a fill-in and taught him to walk like Newhart. Newhart still contends he doesn't walk that way really.

When Newhart won a Peabody Award for *The Bob Newhart Show*, the board said that Newhart was

> *a person whose gentle satire and wry and irreverent wit waft a breath of fresh and bracing air through the stale and stuffy electronic corridors. A merry marauder, who looks less like St. George than a choirboy, Newhart has wounded, if not slain, many of the dragons that stalk our society. In a troubled and apprehensive world, Newhart has proved once again that laughter is the best medicine.*[14]

Lenny Bruce, Dick Gregory and Bob Newhart were bringing a new kind of stand-up to the people of Chicago. Their political and intellectual humor was garnering a whole new audience. Stand-up was on the rise, but its younger counterpart was just getting started. Soon, a new kind of comedy was going to give stand-up a run for its money. Another art form heeded the call of intellectual, political and satirical comedy. What is perhaps the greatest comedy theater of all time was getting ready to grace the stage, and the history of the Second City is a representation of everything that came before it.

9

A STAGE, A CHAIR, A SUGGESTION

We have the luxury and the pleasure of having a glorious failure
also be a glorious success.
—Susan Messing

I t all started with a young woman, Viola Spolin, who worked with the
Works Progress Administration (WPA). The WPA was a national New
Deal program that concentrated on helping the less fortunate. The WPA
focused mainly on finding jobs for the unemployed immigrant women
and children just arriving in Chicago. It offered job training and illiteracy
training and utilized a variety of tactics to assimilate the poor back into the
mainstream. The WPA understood that art can inspire the public, and it let
its artists experiment with their own art forms. The WPA employed tons of
Chicago artists—writers like Nelson Algren, Studs Terkel and Saul Bellow
all contributed their time because it was a chance for the artists to do what
they did best.

The WPA and its artists managed to spawn one of the greatest comedy
movements Chicago had ever seen and, most likely, will ever see again.
At the forefront was Spolin. She got her start in the settlement houses
of Chicago in the 1920s. A settlement house was usually a large, unused
property located in the middle of immigrant neighborhoods. Settlement
workers lived nearby, often on the same property as the people they were
trying to help. It was all about showing the less fortunate that there was a
better life, and it was important that they live this life as well, not just look

at it from the outside. It was common for settlement houses to be located in neighborhoods where few people spoke English, so it was natural that the work being done with women and children involved learning ways around common misunderstandings. As the settlement organizations grew, they contributed to child labor laws, helping with legal problems and building kindergartens and playgrounds.

Hull House, Chicago's first settlement house, was opened by Jane Addams in 1889. Viola Spolin got her start there in 1929 and was heavily influenced by the ideas of Neva Boyd. Boyd also worked at Hull House and was the founder of the Recreational Training School. She was responsible for introducing drama, dancing and play theory to her students. Play theory was the theory that play is an integral part of the human experience. Boyd writes:

> *The spirit of play develops social adaptability, ethics, mental and emotional control, and imagination. These are the more complex adjustments a child learns through play. In play, there are adjustments to new situations constantly. Play experience can prepare the person for purposefulness in non-play activities, for true play creates the incentive to use one's best ability.*[1]

Boyd knew there was a difference between unfocused, chaotic play and play that could be structured to achieve desired goals. This was in a day and age when the attention was on the individual, and if that individual could not succeed, it was their responsibility. Boyd knew the opposite was true.

Spolin worked closely with Boyd, and after getting the job of drama supervisor at the WPA, she started piggybacking on the games presented by Boyd. She put together games based on improvisation, which she would teach to women and children to help assimilate them into the world around them. Spolin had been raised in a family that played lots of games like charades, and she saw the value in learning to communicate in a way that didn't rely so heavily on language. While working at the WPA, Spolin honed the games into something she could easily teach. As one critic put it, Spolin's games were "structures designed to almost fool spontaneity into being."[2] These games were designed to connect people together, to build a "group mind" and to allow people and children to connect on a level they hadn't been used to before.

Spolin's games involved the audience as much as they involved the actors. She was the first to go to the audience for a suggestion, a move that is still a major part of improvisational comedy eighty years later.

Improvisers learning group mind. *Photo courtesy of Angela Manginelli.*

It was also a huge change from the way improvisation had been used before. Burr Tillman improvised and the vaudeville stars improvised, but with the addition of getting a suggestion from the audience, Spolin allowed the audience to see the wonder of "making something up on the spot." Spolin always said of her exercises that her biggest challenge was to help create group mind:

> *The importance of group response, in which players see themselves as an organic part of the whole, becoming one body through which all are directly involved is the outcome of the playing. Being a part of the whole generates trust and frees the player for playing, the many then acting as one.*[3]

When Spolin saw her students stuck on a difficult skill, she would come up with a game to solve that specific problem. Generally, her games focused on getting the who, what and where of every scene. Her other lasting lesson to improvisers everywhere is: "Show, don't tell."

Some of the games Spolin taught during that time were:

CONTACT: Each player must do the scene, but every time they want to speak, they must make physical contact with their scene partner. Touching another player can be frightening, and this exercise is harder than one might think. But it allows the players (the word "actor" was changed to "player" in Spolin's book) to "get out of their head" and concentrate on the task at hand. Once they do that, they lose their inhibitions, and a scene with more intimacy can occur.

BUILDING A STORY: All the players on stage must tell a story in relay fashion, adding on to what the person before has said. This is an exercise that helps build group mind and also aids focus. To keep the story going, each player must be listening to what is going on before them. In the end, the group has created something together, with each player doing his or her part.

Although these games may seem simple when sitting and reading a book describing them, they're actually fairly difficult—but fun. An entirely different muscle is used to focus the mind on the group rather than the individual, and it was precisely that muscle that Spolin was strengthening.

Viola Spolin wasn't the only one experimenting with improv games. Her son, Paul Sills, was enrolled at the University of Chicago in 1948. At that time, the university was a strange and wondrous place. Robert Hutchins took his position as president of the university in 1929. He envisioned the purpose of his university to be "nothing less than to procure a moral, intellectual, and spiritual revolution throughout the world."[4] He hired experienced teachers from all around the world and worked closely with the WPA. Instead of a formal enrollment program, the university offered a series of exams that, if passed, would allow automatic entry into classes. He didn't believe in training his students in useless knowledge but argued that learning to think would enable one to learn how to do.

The university did away with grades and focused on the greater aspects of education. Hutchins even nixed varsity football, claiming it was empty and devoid of purpose. Hutchins's atypical ideals were unsurprisingly labeled as containing threats of "communism" by the famed drugstore owner Charles Walgreen in 1935. Hutchins was accused of communism again in 1949 but stood by his faculty and his school. The threat of communism would hang over the university for years, as the unorthodox school pushed forward. Hutchins left the University of Chicago in 1951, but the reverberations of his actions would last for many years to come. Tim Samuelson agrees that the university was different from most:

> The University of Chicago was always unconventional. It was always experimental and that was the nature of the school. You had the unconventional perspective manifest itself in other places, mainly in what people did as a release.[5]

Paul Sills was a director and theater producer, but the university didn't have its own theater department. So Sills started one. The University Theater was a place where like-minded theater people hung out together. Joining Sills were fellow intellectuals Mike Nichols, Elaine May, Severn Darden and Sheldon Patinkin. In the name of experimentation, Sills taught his fellow theater mates some of his mother's games. Sills used the games to help his actors delve more deeply into group mind and to free up his actors—get them out of their heads.

The University Theater produced and performed scripted, dramatic work, especially the plays of Bertolt Brecht. The plays of Brecht agreed with the intellectual and political ideals of the University Theater. Brecht wanted his plays to inspire political activism rather than just elicit an emotional reaction. His plays would often break the fourth wall to prove to the audience that they were watching a play, much like Garroway used television production to convey the same idea. The old adage of "suspension of disbelief" was not in Brecht's plan. Brecht described it as "stripping the event of its self-evident, familiar, obvious quality and creating a sense of astonishment and curiosity about them."[6] The University Theater morphed into the Playwrights Theater Club, and an unsuspecting alliance was about to take the theater group in an entirely different direction.

David Shepherd was a rich kid from New York City. He studied at Harvard and earned his degree in history of theater from Columbia, but he yearned for a different kind of theater. In the seminal book on the history of Second City, *Something Wonderful Right Away*, Shepherd says:

> *I wanted to rejuvenate the theater. My first love was the theater, which I found had been captured by Giraudoux and Shaw and Ionesco, who would come in and turn it into a distorted picture of life. Instead of being about what's happening in the streets of Chicago, it was about love affairs in Nice which took place fifty years ago. And I thought it was obscene for the theater to be dominated by French and English people. I mean, obscene. I mean, I'm a Yankee. I'm a W.A.S.P. I want a W.A.S.P. theater, OK? And you can't get it on the East Coast because it's dominated by European culture. So you go to the Midwest, which is what I did.[7]*

When Shepherd learned of Sills, there was a natural connection with what he wanted to bring to the theater and what Sills and his group were already working on. Shepherd had wanted to create a theater for the people; he wanted people to come see his theater and sit back, have a drink and a smoke and enjoy watching some satire of what their lives were really like. Sills and his group were working on a more political theater as well. Shepherd figured it was a natural alliance.

Shepherd thought wrong. When it came down to actually working with the company, he complained that its productions were self-centered and bourgeois. Some of his complaints were with the actual plays it was producing. But the 1950s weren't the safest time to speak truths and espouse political activism. Entertainers of all kinds were scared, and the written plays reflected the fear of saying the wrong thing. According to Sheldon Patinkin, one of the founding members of Playwrights:

> *In 1955 we were closed down by the Fire Department for being on the 2nd floor; it was illegal yeah, but we had been there for years. Largely I think it's because we were pink, if not red as the University of Chicago was labeled during those days, and we were doing Brecht and work like that.*[8]

When Playwrights shut down in 1955, Sills and Shepherd started the Compass Players, the cabaret-style show that Shepherd had always dreamed of. He thought if they produced their own plays, had each member of the cast play a variety of characters and kept it fast paced, the general public would stay interested. Shepherd was finally getting the chance he had been waiting for. Patinkin said of Shepherd, "He was the original money at Playwrights, the original money at Compass, and the original producer at both."[9]

While the actors at Playwrights were rehearsing for their scripted pieces, they were still learning and working on improv games with Paul Sills. They were learning the art of improvisation and group mind. And in a move heard around the world, the Compass Players began using the improvisational games to generate material. Improvisation was nothing new, of course. Burr Tillstrom and Fran Bailey did it; Dave Garroway and Studs Terkel did it, too. What was different about the Compass Players was that its actors were not just improvising to get through a television or radio show with no script but used the games purposely, to generate material that could be turned into original material. Currently, almost every sketch show written in the city of Chicago is created using improvisation, but in the 1950s, this was a brand-new idea.

The Compass began to write what it called "scenario plays," loosely based on the old commedia dell'arte format. In commedia, a basic outline was provided, but the material in between was often improvised. At Compass, the scenario plays were structured scenes and beats the actors knew they had to hit, but specific lines and dialogue were improvised.

As the players kept performing their scenario plays, they realized that writing a new one each week was tedious. The group shortened its scenarios and started writing shorter scenes, or sketches. Even though they were intellectuals, the Compass Players actors were relegated back to the bars and saloons of Chicago. Since the bar owner wanted to sell more drinks, he asked the players if they could please make their shows a little longer. But Compass was having a hard enough time writing its scenarios, so instead, to extend the show, the players started improvising after the scripted portion of the show was over. They noticed their audience came for the scenario plays but really stayed for the improvs afterward.

The Compass was changing the way comedy worked. Performing improvisation for its own sake was a bold move; it made the magic trick of improvisation the show in and of itself. This revelation, plus the use of improvisation to generate material, was already a huge paradigm shift. If they had just left it at that, their contribution to comedy would have been unparalleled. But they couldn't leave it at that, could they?

David Shepherd opened a second Compass Players in St. Louis. In Chicago, the Compass Players were concentrating on good scenarios, with slow and patient scene work—the Chicago way. The St. Louis Compass was going for a faster, funnier comedy. The shows would run like this: The players would perform sketches for twenty minutes or so. Then the actors would collect suggestions from the audience. After going backstage to plan out their next moves, the players would come back out and utilize all of the audience suggestions, proving that it had all been made up just a few moments before. Again, there had been improvisation long before the Compass Players, but no one had really pointed out that that's what they were doing.

Playwrights and Compass allowed a great amount of talent to pass through their stages. The experimentation allowed many of the actors, like Shelley Berman, to create their own, distinctive styles of comedy. Mike Nichols and Elaine May developed their hilarious comedy at Playwrights and Compass, and not to repeat the same old story, but they had become so successful that they left Chicago to go seek their fame. On a break from the Big Apple, the two went to St. Louis to check out the latest Compass venture. Nichols and May joined the cast for a bit. The arrival of the two jump-started the St Louis Compass, mostly because of Elaine May. Everyone wanted to play with her. Mike Nichols stayed to play with Compass just so he could continue to be on stage with her. But perhaps May's biggest fan was a young man named Del Close. Close, May and Theodore Flicker (the director of the St. Louis Compass) started to study, in depth, what it was they were doing. They realized they didn't fully understand why some scenes failed and some worked. The three sat down to try to instill some rules, a must when creating a new art form. The rules May, Close and Flicker came up with are rules drilled into the brains of improvisers today:

1. Never deny reality. If an actor establishes something as real, the other actors cannot negate it.
2. Take the active choice. Whenever an actor is faced with a decision during a scene or a game, the actor should always choose the one that will lead to more action.
3. It is the actor's business to justify whatever happens onstage. An actor cannot invent a character that can deny the reality of the scene by claiming it is "out of character." In improvisation, your character is actually you, but with a few additional characteristics.[10]

The basic tenants of improvisation were set down in comedy stone. Essentially, each one of those tenants is encompassed in the phrase "yes and." For many improvisers, "yes and" becomes a way of life, a philosophy of communication at any level. If an actress is on stage and says, "I'm so tired of being pregnant," her fellow actor cannot deny that reality by saying, "But you're not pregnant!" That answer might receive a laugh, but it really stops the scene dead in its tracks. The receiving actor must accept the reality. The "yes" should heighten the statement in return—the "and."

Back in Chicago, the Compass Players had a hard time holding on to a permanent location. After two years in operation, it shut down in 1957. But this was Chicago. One failure—even two failures—mattered not. The spirit of Chicago was to rise again.

Shepherd was out of the picture by this point, frustrated by his stunted dreams. But Sills wasn't even close to finished. He hooked up with Bernie Sahlins and Howard Alk, and on December 16, 1959, the Second City opened in a Chinese laundry in the Old Town neighborhood. Old Town was a hippy artist enclave, known for folk music clubs. It was a perfect home for the Second City for the next fifty years. The first cast of the Second City included Howard Alk, Roger Bowen, Severn Darden, Andrew Duncan, Barbara Troobnick and Mina Kolb. Mike Nichols and Elaine May had left for New York already, ready to show the world the sketches and improvisations they came up with at Compass.

The Second City busts were originally on the Garrick Theater, designed by Louis Sullivan. *Photo courtesy of John Eiberger.*

The name "Second City" came from an article written by A.J. Liebling in 1952. Liebling was a writer from Manhattan who lived what appeared to be a tragic year in Chicago, a city he hated with a passion. He said of Chicago, "Seen from the taxi, on the long ride in from the airport, the place looked slower, shabbier and, in defiance of all chronology, older than New York."[11] The former Compass Players took the insult as its name, effectively proving Liebling wrong about what he considered to be a very self-conscious city.

Bernie Sahlins, one of the original founders, said of the early days:

> *We came up at a strange period, McCarthyism; it was a period of repression and people wouldn't dare, they were telling mother-in-law jokes, and then the long week came and Lenny Bruce and Dick Gregory upset the applecart. Anything we did was a political statement; it was important. People would shiver when you said "shit" on stage; it was a period of repression and we un-repressed it.*[12]

Second City was popular right away. It may not have been the audience Shepherd had been looking for, but there was an audience. Playwrights and Compass had grown a nice following during the early years, and fellow university students composed most of the audience. The actors were highly intelligent and highly referential and spoofed everything from literature to politics to random pieces of extraordinary knowledge. Chicago loved Second City even though improvisation and the scenes that came from it were never a sure thing. An improv could be hilarious, or it could be horrible, and it's this dichotomy that made Chicago such a safe place to try it out. Bernie Sahlins said:

> *Chicago is different because it's not on a coast. It's different from New York or LA because you have the right to fail, you get more than one chance. This right to fail is very important and the right to start again. New York audiences are looking at the stage and when it's time to laugh they look around to see if its okay. Chicagoans react to what they see; we like it or we don't like it. We're not so much for fashion.*[13]

Although Second City was immune to the classic problem of drumming up an audience, it still had to deal with the ongoing battle Chicago has always fought: losing actors to New York. Mike Nichols and Elaine May had left the nest, and more were still to come. Sills and company were producing such fine comedic actors that it was no surprise these versatile players were being hired in other major cities.

The biggest hit came in 1975 with the premiere of *Saturday Night Live*. Second City was on a roll; it had some of the greatest comedians, all settling into the Second City lifestyle. But when *SNL* premiered, the new cast consisted of Dan Aykroyd, John Belushi, Chevy Chase, Jane Curtin, Garrett Morris, Laraine Newman, Gilda Radner, George Coe and Michael O'Donoghue. Aykroyd, Belushi and Gilda were all from the Second City. In a way, it would hurt the theater because the exact thing that was making it successful was being taken away year after year. But the success and fame of the actors solidified the notion that the Second City was the biggest name in comedy. The Second City was *it*, and the institution wasn't about to go anywhere.

John Belushi is probably the most well-known Chicagoan to have graced the stages of Second City. Born in Chicago, Belushi was raised in Wheaton. In college, Belushi started an improv group called the West Compass Players. The name of his group left no doubt about who his greatest influences were. After moving to the Circle Campus at the University of Illinois, Belushi was performing more than ever. Joyce Sloane, a producer at Second City, saw him perform and said, "Hey, you stole the Second City material anyway, you might as well come to the theater."[14] Belushi did and was hired by the Second City. He performed in his first show in 1971. He broke the mold by being the first person hired who never went through the Second City Training Center. That's because Belushi was pure—a true student of improvisation. He was a natural, never afraid of the stage and of improvisation like so many before him. Harold Ramis, a former performer at Second City, said of Belushi, "John brought a street element...[that] cut through the intellectual pretense of the theater. He brought rock and roll to the show."[15]

Belushi took one for the team when it came to getting *The Blues Brothers* made in Chicago. In 1979, Belushi paid a visit to Mayor Jane Byrne while Dan Aykroyd cowered in the lobby outside her office. Belushi was understandably nervous. Chicago, under the previous mayor, Richard J. Daley, had not been a friendly place to make movies. Things might have been different had Dick Gregory beat him, but Daley feared that movies made in Chicago would highlight the gangs or the mob, so he was never supportive of making movies in the city. But Chicago had a new mayor, and Belushi sucked it up and went into her office. He was sweating, nervous and talked a mile a minute. Byrne knew from the beginning that she was going to let him make the movie but enjoyed watching the poor guy sweat it out a little bit. Once he got the thumbs up, Belushi, Aykroyd and John

Second City alums Tina Fey and Adam McKay were both hired as head writers for *Saturday Night Live*. *Photo courtesy of Fuzzy Gerdes.*

Landis made their love letter to Chicago. The movie showcased Chicago, making many parts of the city (including the chase scene through Daley Plaza) familiar to people all over the world. *The Blues Brothers* did for Chicago what Belushi did for Second City: made it cool.

John Belushi owed a lot of his success to his favorite teacher, Del Close. Close got his start with the Compass Players in St. Louis. Then a young man, Del was crazy—a mad genius. He was one of those men who is so smart, it's to his detriment. His mind was a big place to play, and Del used drugs to quiet that brain. Del eventually came in as a director for Second City, taking over for Bernie Sahlins. Del was always a great teacher, but as a director, he was a little messy. He would be in the middle of setting up a new show and then would unexpectedly walk out the door, leaving everyone in the lurch. Through the years, Del struggled with alcohol, speed and marijuana. He believed that drugs would open his creative mind and allow him to find the mysteries of what it meant to be a human being. Del hung out with the other sick comedians. He hung out with Lord Buckley and Lenny Bruce and was influenced by their comedy. Del even tried his hand at stand-up and produced a comedy album titled *How to Speak Hip*. It achieved modest success.

Although a brilliant and hilarious performer, Del was not easy to work with. Sheldon Patinkin, who was directing Second City at the time, tells of one scary night with Del Close. Del had made one of what would be many suicide attempts by swallowing pills right before a show. He called the theater and told people there what he'd done. Patinkin ran over to Del's apartment, looked through the window and saw Del lying on the floor. Scared out of his mind, Patinkin raced back to the theater and grabbed Bernie Sahlins and together they broke into Del's apartment. They hurried Del to the hospital, where doctors pumped his stomach and stabilized him. The hospital wanted to admit him, but Second City's lawyer found a doctor who ran a clinic on the south side. After Del was there about a month, the doctor said Del could continue to do shows if someone would pick him up and drop him off right after the show. This job fell to Patinkin, and Del, always the rebel, resented him for it. Patinkin, in turn, resented Del, and although there was some level of respect on both sides, Del's relationships at Second City started to decline. Del's drug use wasn't fun for anyone, including Del. Patinkin recalls one night:

> *I had a little tab of LSD that I was going to try and before I tried it, Del called and said, "Would you come over and sit with me, I'm being devoured inch by inch by a spider king." Needless to say, I flushed the tab down the toilet.*[16]

Jack McBrayer left Second City to costar on *30 Rock* as Kenneth the Page. *Photo courtesy of the Chicago Improv Festival and Angela Manginelli.*

Del's other drug was improvisation. Always searching for the answers to the mysteries of the human mind, Del used improv to help his search. After hard years with the Second City, Del would come to believe that improvisation was not just a tool to generate material but was also an art form in and of itself. He wanted to explore the darker sides of it, the mystical sides. Eventually, Del left Second City. Whether he was fired, let go or quit, it really doesn't matter. Del was finished with the Second City.

Second City is still a major jumping-off point for improvisers looking for fame. *Saturday Night Live* just recently hired four Chicagoans. Shows like *The Daily Show* and *The Colbert Report* (Colbert was also on the Second City main stage, along with fellow funnyman Steve Carell) regularly come to the theater to scout talent. Just like after the fire, when all the great architects came to Chicago to build, after Second City laid the groundwork, people came. And it's no wonder. At the newly expanded Second City Training Center, one of its current two thousand students can learn how to write, direct and play in the Second City style.

Second City recently celebrated its fiftieth anniversary, and the list of famous alumni can be seen both in and outside the theater. Tina Fey, Jack McBrayer, Bill Murray, Gilda Radner, Chris Farley and Dan Aykroyd are some of the faces that stare accusingly at hopeful students passing through the theater's halls. Second City helped Chicago actors create a group mind and write and perform together. It energized the theater scene in Chicago. Before Second City, there weren't any small, independent theaters, or "black box" theaters. Along with a relaxed fire code law in the 1970s that made it easier for storefront theaters to dot the horizon, Second City helped create a community of theaters that total over two hundred today. Its footprint in Chicago was set; the mecca was made. Second City may have been king, but its prodigal prince was longing to break away.

10

TRUTH IN COMEDY

It was always about doors opening for me. Del was the doorway.
—*Charna Halpern*

The story of how someone gets into the world of comedy in Chicago usually starts the same way: You go to a party and meet some people who have been doing comedy already. You joke and laugh with them and realize there are no other people on earth like these. And that's it. You're hooked.

It happened that way for Charna Halpern, too. She went to a party with a friend and met some Second City people there. Charna jumped in and did bits with the rest of them but thought nothing of it. Later that night, Second City actor Tim Kazurinsky told Charna he thought she was funny and that she should audition for Second City. He called Joyce Sloane, and Charna found herself auditioning for the main stage. She did her best, but she knew she didn't know what she was doing. Later that night, she went to see a show at Second City and understood completely. Once she took classes, she was hooked. But it wasn't just the comedy that she loved; she was a natural leader. She was the one who scheduled rehearsals and got gigs for her new improv group Standard Deviations.

Charna heard that David Shepherd was coming to Second City. She, like every new improviser, had read Jeffrey Sweet's *Something Wonderful Right Away*. She recalled reading that David Shepherd had tried something called Improv Olympic—a competition where improv teams would compete against one another:

I'm on the highway going home, and I'll never forget this because it was the first major revelation I've ever had in my life. I was on the highway thinking, "David Shepherd, what did I read about him; he did this thing in Canada called Improv Olympic but it didn't go." And I thought, I can do this, I can get David Shepherd to start Improv Olympic here, and I swear to god this is the revelation: I'm going to run iO, this is what I'm going to do, this is my life. This is my job. I knew it. I got on the cloverleaf and went back downtown and never made it home.[1]

Shepherd was in. But after a few fits and starts, some of which left Charna in the lurch, she pressed Shepherd to let her continue with Improv Olympic here in Chicago, and he could do it in New York or wherever. He acquiesced, and Improv Olympic became the domain of Charna Halpern.

Charna found a space at Crosscurrents, a theater on Belmont and Wilton, a section of town where punk met runaway and runaway met high school kids from the well-to-do North Shore of Chicago. Charna held improv competitions, and she was good at it. She put together theme teams, like the team of all policemen or psychologists (the Freudian Slippers). She did well courting the media, but eventually the gamey-ness of what she was doing started to gnaw at her. She knew there must be something different out there.

Charna Halpern and Tina Fey. *Photo courtesy of Fuzzy Gerdes.*

Charna knew about Del Close, and apparently Del knew a bit about Charna, enough to call her a twit behind her back anyway. Charna heard Del was performing an invocation at an art gallery for Halloween. She went to the gallery to check it out and was horrified to see Del doing an invocation. Charna was into meditation at the time and had recently studied how to protect herself with a "white light" against evil spirits. Here was Del calling up gods and demons without protecting anyone. The petite Charna Halpern stormed up to the hulking Del Close and told him, "You have a lot of nerve invoking demons. No one in here is protected!"

Del said, "I protected the whole building!"

"You can't do that," she protested.

"Yes I can!"

Charna stormed out, thinking to herself, "What an asshole, now I don't like him either."[2]

The idea that something more was out there nagged at Halpern. Long-form improvisation wasn't happening in the city at the time. Second City was writing material generated from improvisation, and the Player's Workshop, a training center connected to Second City, was still teaching mainly games. Charna's instinct led her to seek out Del one more time. She figured he wouldn't remember what had happened at the art gallery months earlier; he was probably messed up on drugs anyway. Charna offered Del $200 and some pot to teach a class at one of her workshops. He asked, "What am I going to have to do for it?"

"Whatever you want," she answered.

With a smirk on his face, he said, "Can I invoke demons?" Del remembered.

That night, Del Close taught his first workshop at Improv Olympic. Charna was floored. Del revealed secrets of the universe. After the workshop, Del and Charna went out for coffee. She told him she wanted something more, and he mentioned that he had something he'd been working on for years. He said if she would like to close her "little game theater," then he would come teach at her theater. In 1983, Del and Charna joined forces, and long-form improvisation was ready to make itself known at every bar that had anything resembling a stage.

Del believed in improvisation as an art form. Improvisation was not just a tool for writing or freeing up actors or children, but it could stand on its own. For years, Del had toyed with a form called Harold. The name means nothing, but the form changed everything. Del wanted something he could teach, a form of improvisation that the people would watch and find interesting. Charna had amassed a crew of people who had gone through classes at Second City and wanted something else to learn. Charna said of Del's workshops:

> *It was always about doors opening for me. He would say, "I'll tell you what, you're at a scene in a restaurant, the president has just been shot... don't talk about it. We want to see it." Or "You're in a living room and someone is having wild sex in the bedroom, don't talk about it."* [3]

Charna was blown over, and the scenes were so much more intense. It was a whole different vibe than watching quick-fire games.

Harold came out of Del's time in San Francisco, when he was working with a group called the Committee in the 1960s. Harold was a loose form in which scenes would be introduced, characters from one scene would float into another and scenes and themes would tie into one another. It was hard to teach, and it was hard to do. Even though Del despised many of the games involved with improvisation at the time, one of them caught his eye. Time Dash was a Spolin game that allowed the characters in one scene to move either forward or backward in time to give a greater insight into the characters. Del figured he could use that game to help give Harold some form. The addition of Time Dash helped Del and Charna figure out a way to give Harold some structure and make it something they could actually teach.

The essential structure of a Harold is similar to a *Seinfeld* episode: The players get a suggestion from the audience, and the Harold begins with a group game, something that allows the suggestion to sink in and generate a variety of themes. Then the scenes start. Two players come out for scene 1A, two more players for 1B and then two more for 1C. Three scenes have been introduced. The next time we see these characters, the Time Dash will be employed, and we see characters again at a different point in the future or past, scenes 2A, 2B and 2C. Then there will be another group game, and the last three scenes will (hopefully) tie in together in a beautiful and wonderful mess of improvisation. Harold is not easy. It's actually quite difficult and takes massive amounts of focus. It really does work all the muscles an improviser needs: focus, memory and innovation.

Once Harold was given form and could be taught and performed by players on every level, iO blew up. Originally called Improv Olympic, the Olympic committee eventually came after Halpern and told her she would not able to use the word Olympic in her business name. Classes were filling up, and Charna needed to structure a more formal training center. Everyone was coming to learn from "guru" Del Close. Charna tamed and took care of Del, and Del tamed performers. He taught his students to be more in control and to play the truth of the moment. Charna used to hear him say, "You have to care about yourself but you have to care about the art more than yourself. Love your art, not you in the art."

Halpern made another move when she started putting students on stage. Second City only had the main stage and its second theater, the e.t.c. If an improviser didn't get cast there, that was it—no more stage time. Sure, there were always bars to do shows in, but nothing beats a stage. At iO, people got stage time—real stage time—in front of a paying audience. With so much more opportunity to be on stage than at Second City, iO became the place to go for people who wanted to learn improvisation as an art form, learn from the guru and, as a bonus, get a great social life.

Del was a great teacher to so many and a so-so teacher to some. Del did not suffer fools well. If a student decided to go for the dirty joke in a scene—or tried for a laugh at all—that student could very well be expelled from class, in front of the whole class, and might never be allowed back into class ever again. Women claimed to have felt the ire of Del more than their male counterparts. Complaints about his misogynistic ways were common.

Susan Messing proves that women are funny—and hungry. *Photo courtesy of Ken Manthey.*

Del Close and Charna Halpern. *Photo courtesy of Charna Halpern.*

Yet there are just as many women who learned so much from Del and never had a problem. Susan Messing, from the Annoyance, Second City and everywhere else, said, "I didn't care if Del hated women. It didn't matter, because he loved me; so yes, he might have been absolutely misogynistic and I didn't give a shit."[4] Tina Fey had much the same thing to say. When asked if Del liked women, Fey said:

> *I don't think Del liked anybody. Obviously he was so good to Charna over the years and they were so close. I think...Del didn't like bad improvisers of a very specific sort, which was soft, timid, cute—which probably, more bad women improvisers fell into that category. Whereas bad male improvisers fall into the category of never shutting up and entering every scene, trying to be funny, so maybe that irritated him less...everyone puts that through their own filters, and if you were a woman and he told you you suck, then you might say that he hates women, but you probably need to explore the possibility that maybe you do suck.*[5]

Comedy has always been considered a boys' club. But according to Susan Messing, things are changing:

> *I think in Chicago it's starting to become a moot point; people don't even have to have this conversation. I think it's hard for women in other cities because they don't have the day-to-day mantra "that's a moot point, get over it, things are unfair who cares." Too many women are doing extremely well now so we've proven women are funny. I think that it's very evolved in Chicago and I think that other women are hungry for this information.*[6]

Charna Halpern summed it up best when she was asked about Chicago comedy being a boys' club: "I didn't even know there was a club."[7]

Del passed away in 1999 from emphysema. His last turn would be to donate his skull to the Goodman Theater to be featured in upcoming productions of *Hamlet*. iO continues on without him. His students now teach the influx of new improvisers converging on iO. Halpern continues to grow her theater and graduate students who find work all over the world; people like Tina Fey, Chris Farley and Amy Poehler all learned from Del and iO, and more are surely yet to come. When asked what had changed since Del's death, Charna replied, "The thing that changed was my life, my adventure. Things got a lot more boring without him around."[8]

11

IT GOES UP TO ELEVEN

In Chicago you have the opportunity to grow; you don't get stunted before you have
that chance. You can have that set back and say, what did I learn from that?
—*Mark Sutton*

Now that Chicago improvisers had teachers and forms and rules, it didn't take long for a group to come along and break them. Mick Napier moved to Chicago in 1987 after graduating from Indiana University. In college, Napier, Joe Bill and Mark Henderson put an improv group together. After reading *Something Wonderful Right Away* and seeing all of one Second City show, Napier and his friends taught themselves how to improvise. After he graduated from college, Napier moved to Chicago and started putting on shows at Crosscurrents, the same bar where Halpern was holding her classes. Metraform, as the group was known then, opened a show called *Splatter Theater* in 1987. Like most excellent ideas, the brainstorm for *Splatter Theater* occurred over beers on a particularly saucy evening. Napier wanted to create a parody of the old gore flicks. Taking the reins from what the players learned at Second City, Metraform wrote out a basic scenario, the only qualifier being use as much blood as possible. The show was not for the faint of heart: "Some of the stage effects included a nun getting drilled in the back of the head, a bimbo getting her tongue ripped out and a policeman having his intestines removed."[1] Believe it or not, *Splatter Theater* was very highly reviewed.

Joe Bill, Mick Napier and Mark Sutton—the bad boys of comedy. *Photo courtesy of Ken Manthey.*

After Crosscurrents closed, Metraform found a permanent theater on Broadway and Belmont and changed its name from Metraform (not very subversive) to the Annoyance (more subversive). After the high from the success of its first show and new theater, it opened *Splatter Theater Two*, which unfortunately was not quite as well reviewed as the first one. The Annoyance lost a lot of money from those bad reviews. But this is Chicago, after all, and the newly named Annoyance gave it one more shot. Napier gave his thoughts on what the next show should be: "This is all I know: I know that I want this show to be a musical. I want it to be vile and dirty and disgusting and at some point, I want a guy in a dress to fight a clown and I want my dog in it."[2] Little did Mick Napier, Mark Sutton or Joe Bill know, but *Co-Ed Prison Sluts* would become the longest-running original musical in Chicago.

Although *Co-Ed* was created through improvisation, much like how Second City wrote its shows, it was the epitome of the Annoyance aesthetic. The show was littered with swear words. It was dirty but hilarious; smart but incredibly silly. It put the Annoyance and its bad boy image on the map. They definitely weren't doing shows like this at iO or the Second City.

The Annoyance was having a hard time with its theater. The players were inexperienced when they rented it and ended up owing money for taxes. They needed a new theater and found one in Wrigleyville, just steps from Halpern's iO.

The next show, *The Real Live Brady Bunch*, proved that the Annoyance wasn't just a flash in the pan. The show was filled with spot-on impressions of the Brady kids and referenced every classic scene. With *Co-Ed* secure and the *Brady Bunch* running sold-out shows on an off night, the Annoyance was able to keep stretching and playing with other forms. Napier had learned and performed the Harold at iO, but just like Halpern before him, he knew there was something else out there. The Annoyance became the place to do all the things the other theaters wouldn't let you do. It was the embodiment of the Chicago axiom of it being okay to fail. Napier says:

> *Shows like these were not so much born from the desire to be radical, as they were more a consequence of the invitation to do whatever you want on stage. Our work is uncensored. The only censorship is self-imposed, and the criterion of that censorship is whether or not the content fulfils the mission of the show.*[3]

Marcia and Cindy from *The Real Live Brady Bunch. Photo courtesy of Ken Manthey.*

The Annoyance started holding classes as well. Once students had learned the rules of improv from iO and Second City, the Annoyance was the place to go to learn to break them. The common denominator of the rules of improv boils down to taking care of your scene partner. Group mind essentially means make your partner look good. The Annoyance had a different rule: make sure when you get up on stage that you have something for yourself, a wish, a secret or a line of dialogue. Just like the oxygen mask on the planes, once you're secure, it makes it that much easier to help your scene partner. The Annoyance continued creating and writing shows through improvisation. Perhaps some of the titles will shed some light on their productions: *Your Butt, Tippi: Portrait of a Teenage Virgin* and *Manson: The Musical.*

In the new age of serious and philosophical long-form improvisation taught by Del Close, it was the players at ComedySportz who were the real rebels. While Del taught "no jokes, no bits," ComedySportz did exactly that. ComedySportz started in 1985 in Milwaukee. Based on the techniques of Keith Johnstone and his book, *Impro*, ComedySportz took the basics of improvisation—the games—and started to delve deeper into how to play them for an audience. Johnstone used improvisation to go more deeply into scene study and characters; he applied the concepts of improvisation to the theater. Johnstone took it one step further and created Theatresports, which was basically playing improv games in front of an audience, taking suggestions and using those suggestions in a competition format. Only in Theatersports, gags and one-liners were frowned upon. It was about storytelling and group mind. ComedySportz was born out of Theatersports but concentrated more heavily on the competition aspect of the game, even utilizing a referee to make sure all players were playing the game correctly. ComedySportz welcomed gags and one-liners as long as they came as quickly as possible.

ComedySportz Chicago opened in 1987 and has since moved over fourteen times. This is a major accomplishment for the group, which has stayed in business despite all the location changes. Audiences are loyal to ComedySportz and will follow it all over the city. Part of the reason people love it so much is because it's accessible, understandable and moves quickly, so if one scene is off, the next one is right around the corner. Like they say about Chicago weather, "If you don't like it, wait fifteen minutes." ComedySportz steered away from the long-form improvisation that Del had made so popular at iO. Del would always say to not go for the joke, but at ComedySportz, the opposite is true. Instead of searching for the truth of the scene, the players look for the joke of the scene. It's not theatrical or dramatic, but it's funny, and it moves at lightning pace.

Anything could happen at a ComedySportz show. *Photo courtesy of the Chicago Improv Festival and Jerry Schulman.*

In Chicago, there has always been a philosophical battle between long form and short form over whether one is more pure than the other. ComedySportz doesn't care much for pure; it's just trying to make people laugh. And unlike its bad boy friends at the Annoyance, players aren't allowed to use dirty or blue jokes. Dave Gaudet, one of the early members of ComedySportz, says, "We're the only show doing short form. Audiences can get it instantly; it's accessible and it's clean, so you can bring your family. There are people that used to come here in grade school and now they're bringing their kids."[4] ComedySportz, unlike the Annoyance, the Playground and others, wasn't created to fill a void that Second City or iO left unfilled. It came from a whole different direction than Spolin and Del. Gaudet says, "For years people have said, 'We're doing art and you're going for the laugh,' but it's comedy, so yes, we would agree with that sentiment. Where's the bad part?"[5]

Don Hall, a former member of ComedySportz and founder of WNEP Theater, put it this way:

> *Improvisers can't handle a lot of games, which I think is to their detriment. I've always said if your gig is "I want to go through the schooling," what you do is you go to ComedySportz, take their classes and learn how to play games faster than anybody. You can bitch about ComedySportz, but no one plays those games faster and better than those people. If you can learn to do that, that's a skill you now have in your bag.*[6]

ComedySportz also has a training center and a permanent home in a space on Belmont and Clark, an area that is quickly becoming "Comedy Row." Besides Second City, ComedySportz is one of the only theaters that doesn't struggle eternally for an audience. So many improv theaters either struggle to bring in their own audience or perform mainly for other improvisers. There's nothing wrong with this scenario, but ComedySportz has been about bringing short form improvisation to the people.

Second City classes end at Level 5. Back in the day, before the glut of improv training centers opened up, after finishing Level 5 there was nowhere else to go. Another group that came out of the need for a Level 6 at Second City was WNEP, which stands for "What No One Else Produces." Having finished Level 5 at Second City, students Don Hall and Joe Janes still wanted someplace to play. They started their

WNEP's *Dada* players look at themselves in Cloud Gate at Millennium Park. *Photo courtesy of Fuzzy Gerdes.*

own theater and experimented with form and a more theatrical-based improvisation. Don Hall thought about what he wanted to produce: "I'm going to do something that allows me to do whatever the hell I want. I'll surround myself with the funniest, weirdest people I know and let them do whatever they want, and we'll see what happens."[7] The Chicago style wins out again.

When Hall started the theater, he called Andrew Alexander, CEO and co-owner of Second City, Mick Napier and even Del Close to ask for help. Everyone was completely helpful:

> *Everyone was awesome, everyone was open, everyone was giving and everyone had great advice. The thing about it at the time, and I think that's still the case, is there wasn't a sense of competition. At that time, Chicago comedy was really just stand-up. It was sort of the transition period, because Chicago comedy went from 80s' stand-up and improv is for dumbasses to the 90s being very much improv and stand-up being lame, and now it's flipped again.*[8]

The Playground builds a stage for its black box theater. *Photo courtesy of John Eiberger.*

They did shows like *Soriée Dada: Blinde Esel Hopse, My Grandmother Is a Fat Whore from Jersey* and *Metaluna*. WNEP is known for playing with various forms, like improvising around an obituary or sending out white-faced Dadaists into the city. They give in to their fantasies and have quickly grown to become one of the most eclectic theater companies in Chicago.

Just as iO grew out of the backlash from Second City, so many other theaters grew out of the backlash from iO. One of those theaters, the Playground, became a place where rules and a ruling artistic director were out of business. The first not-for-profit improv co-op of its kind, the Playground was a place to play where no one judged, no one was watching and teams could feel free to try out any form they liked. After moving theaters a few times (finding the pattern yet?), the Playground ended up in the same theater previously occupied by WNEP.

Many other theaters such as pH Productions, Chemically Imbalanced Comedy and the Laugh Out Loud Theater in Schaumburg have opened in response to needing additional places to play. These are the small, black theaters that have become such an important part of the improv scene. As these theaters break away from the big guns at Second City or iO, they experiment with the rules and basics of improv, creating more forms and more experienced players.

While Second City, the Annoyance and iO were competing in the friendly improv wars, a completely different kind of war was raging in the stand-up comedy clubs. Just as television shows like *Saturday Night Live* had a direct effect on improv and sketch theaters in Chicago, cable TV would change everything for the stand-up comic and for the comedy clubs in Chicago.

12

THE PAPER WARS

Chicago is a great place to do stand-up. The audiences are receptive and intelligent; they're skeptical but cynical.
—*Bert Haas*

Lenny Bruce, Dick Gregory and Bob Newhart did their part in making stand-up comedy its own art. Through the 1960s, stand-up was about telling the truth, about finding a voice and about revolution and freedom of speech. In 1975, stand-up underwent a new revolution when HBO gave Robert Klein his first comedy concert special. People fell in love with stand-up comedy; it was suddenly accessible to everyone. Now people could see their favorite comedian on TV and then go see that same famous person at one of the sixteen stand-up clubs that sprouted up in Chicago. According to Bert Haas, executive vice-president at Zanies Comedy Club:

> *Everything came together, and it created this great awareness for stand-up comedy and this great market for it too. And of course what always happens in America is there's a market for it and everybody piles on and it becomes the boom or the bubble.*[1]

The bubble did indeed arrive, and stand-up clubs were all the rage. The clubs in the late 1980s and early '90s were huge, harkening back to the old days at the Sauganash. Comedy clubs like the Improv or the

Funny Firm could hold four or five hundred people, and they were right down the street from each other. For a while, people were happy to pay big money and their two-drink minimum to see the headliners they saw on television. Stand-up comics were mainstream, and they became a business.

As stand-up comedy became more prevalent on cable TV, the general public realized they could watch their favorite comedians from their comfy couches and not have to pay the amount of money they would need to in a club. Unlike improv comedy, which still has never been able to successfully move to television (with the exception of *Whose Line Is It Anyway*), stand-up translated quite well. The clubs in Chicago were hurting. They had these huge rooms to fill, they were paying their star comedians a ton of money and people chose to watch comedy from the comfort of their own homes. As some clubs started to close, other clubs tried a variety of methods to fill up their huge spaces. And so began the comedy club "Paper Wars."

The Funny Firm started using telemarketing to "paper" its shows. Some nice young man would call from lists of former clubgoers and offer customers up to ten free tickets on an off night. They knew the money was in the bar anyway; if they could get people in the door with free tickets, they could move their drinks no problem. By day, these huge rooms would be filled with tables, chairs, phones and huge stacks of paper with phone numbers on them. Maybe it worked for a little while, but what ended up happening was it cheapened the club, the show and the comedians. It cheapened everything, and the whole experience changed. Now that people were getting into the clubs for free, it didn't mean anything anymore. Audiences were getting drunker, security guards had to be hired and the comedians were getting heckled and booed but were still expecting the same paychecks as before. Bert Haas remembered one night:

> *I was working the door here* [at Zanies] *one night and I get a page from the box office that there's a call for me. They tell me it's John at the Funny Firm. And I think, okay, it must be the manager I don't know. I get on the phone and I hear, "Hey! I just wanted to say congratulations! You've just won eight free tickets to the Funny Firm!" I said, "Do you know who you're calling?" "Yes, I'm calling Zanies, and you won eight tickets for a Thursday show!" So I play him, "You know what, John, I can't make it tomorrow night. Any chance I could use them on*

Saturday?" He said, "Well we normally don't do that, but since you're a winner, what show were you interested in on Saturday?"[2]

Haas went on to explain that it's just not a viable business model. People who didn't understand the business jumped on the bandwagon, and out of the sixteen clubs that existed in the Chicagoland area, about six are left. Three of those are Zanies. Zanies stayed in business by keeping an intimate room, paying the comics a reasonable amount and, most importantly, never papering their house. According to Haas, "We took a beating for a couple of years, because obviously people went to where it was free. We held the line with talent, and we held the line with quality. We said this is what we do, win or lose."[3]

The clubs on the south side of Chicago were fighting their own battles. The premier club, All Jokes Aside, started on the south side in 1992 after the boom had already hit. At that time, the majority of stand-up clubs in Chicago were on the north side and catered to white comedians and white audiences. James Alexander and Raymond Lambert saw that there was a huge demand for black comics after *Showcase at the Apollo* premiered in 1987 and the *Def Comedy Jam* in 1992. Together with Mary Lindsey, they opened All Jokes Aside to showcase up-and-coming black talent.

The club did well during the heyday, showcasing comedians like Bernie Mac, who grew up on the south side and would put on shows for kids in his neighborhood. After playing All Jokes Aside and appearing on *Def Comedy Jam*, Mac shot to fame and helped bring the club publicity. The club hosted such greats as Chris Tucker, Mo'Nique and Dave Chapelle. The thing was, Alexander and Lambert weren't from Chicago and didn't realize how segregated Chicago really was. All Jokes Aside became known as a club for only black comedians and black audiences. Any thoughts of expanding to the north side and attracting a white audience were thwarted. They closed the club less than a decade after they opened it.

Mary Lindsey wasn't quite finished, however. In 2006, Lindsey opened Jokes and Notes in the Bronzeville neighborhood. Brian Babylon, a regular at Jokes and Notes, says the community is still really segregated but that white comics from the north side are learning to play the black clubs and vice versa:

Dion Cole, he's like…my role model. He said you gotta figure out a way to make your joke be funny to the same people. It's all about likeability; once people like you, they'll let you say anything. Get 'em on your side and then go to town.[4]

Hannibal Buress. *Photo courtesy of Fuzzy Gerdes.*

But Jokes and Notes isn't getting stuck in the same rut as All Jokes Aside. The club attracts white comedians and a white audience. If a north side comic can have a great night at Jokes and Notes, then he knows he's getting good. Up-and-coming comics like Hannibal Buress, who was hired to write for *Saturday Night Live* and then *30 Rock*, learned to play both sides of town. Bert Haas of Zanies was amazed by Buress's passion:

> *I love Hannibal. When he was in Chicago, he got on stage every night. Every night he found a stage to perform on. He never owned a car. I don't know how he got to the gigs every night. I always say to the new talent, I don't want to hear your excuses. Hannibal didn't even have a car and he found stages and he worked.*[5]

Perhaps Babylon put the difference between south side and north side comedy best when he said, "The north side will get you famous, the south side will get you paid."[6]

And so the seesaw continues. Stand-up is king, improv goes down; then improv is king, and stand-up goes down. But the fact remains, in stand-up, in improvisation and in sketch, Chicago is the place to come for comedy. Conan, Colbert, Jon Stewart, *Saturday Night Live* and a multitude of sitcoms scout out comedians in Chicago.

13

THE BRIDGE

Chicago is known for slow, patient, grounded scene work, and you're true to the characters and true to the relationship. That seems to be the impression of what the Chicago style is.
—Jonathan Pitts

C hicago was the mecca, but there was still something missing. One phenomenon of improvisation, sketch and even stand-up comedy was the introduction of the comedy festival. In the late 1990s, festivals were happening all around the country. These festivals were held in Kansas City, Austin, Miami—smaller cities where they hungered for knowledge. People were brought together through workshops, shows, lectures and, of course, parties. The days of Mick Napier learning to improvise by reading a book and seeing one Second City show were over. Now the Chicago comedians would travel the country, teaching college kids, and anyone else who was interested, how to do comedy the Chicago way. Halpern said, "Even if you're a B level here, if you go somewhere else, you're the best. So, when there are festivals, if you don't have a Chicago team, you don't have a festival."[1] The word was spreading.

Yet up until 1998, the home of comedy didn't have a festival of its own. Jonathan Pitts and Frances Callier stepped up to the challenge, and the Chicago Improv Festival (CIF) was born. Pitts explained why he thought he was the right person to start this festival:

CIF's College Comedy Championship. *Photo courtesy of the Chicago Improv Festival and Angela Manginelli.*

> *When I first started CIF, I called the other theaters the mafia family, and I think that's part of the reason why no one had done this before. Back then, if one theater started the festival, they wouldn't have gotten such warm support from the others. We were neutral, and with me not being in the community for a while because I was doing theater and performance art, it created space. I was in Second City. I was at iO. Dave Gaudet and I auditioned for ComedySportz together, so I had connections with everyone and I saw the value in everyone.*[2]

The Chicago Improv Festival is currently in its fourteenth year, and even though it's been through many changes, those changes reflect how comedy is evolving. Pitts is not only interested in showcasing the great improvisation that happens in Chicago, but he is also committed to bringing improvisation to the rest of the world. He's added an international component to the festival and remarks, "It's amazing to see how other people create theater and how other people do it. Even though we don't share the same language, we share the same ideas."[3]

Pitts has expanded the scope of CIF as well. Along with the annual improv festival held every spring, Pitts has created a College Improv Tournament, a Teen Comedy Fest and an educational outreach program, all designed to be bridges for young comedians to cross before they play with the big boys.

14

BACK TO THE FUTURE

No one ever expected this to happen.
—Joyce Sloane

Where does the improv and stand-up world stand now? Second City has roughly two thousand students going through its classes at any one time and iO has eight hundred students. The fear now is oversaturation and whether anything new can come out of Chicago. The rebels of yesterday have become the institutions of today. Second City has its way of performing, iO has its way, ComedySportz has its and the Annoyance has its. One wonders where there is space for a new way of comedy.

Almost everyone agrees that Chicago is now on the map. Stand-ups and improvisers are getting work in Hollywood, and casting agents across the country are recommending training time in Chicago for their actors. Students flock here from all over the world to learn from the best. But what's next?

Of course, no one knows what the next step is or they'd be taking it. But the dividing line between stand-up comedy and improvisation and sketch has always been a bold one. It was rare for comedians to cross that line. Stand-ups perform at Zanies on the north side or at Jokes and Notes on the south side. There are multitudes of open mic nights all over the city. Improvisers perform at one of the "big four" and race to their next shows at one of the others. But as comedians start hitting the wall on what they're learning, it seems as if the two forms are starting to mix. Shows like *The Moth* bring stand-up and improvisation together through storytelling competitions. In countless bars across the city, people are coming together for shows like *Paper Machete* or *Essay Fiesta*, which mix stand-up, improvisation and entertainment.

Second City, as of this writing, is expanding its theater. The Lakeshore Theater, a large comedy venue on the north side that closed a few years ago, is preparing to be another stand-up club. New black box comedy theaters are opening every day, and the people continue to pour into Chicago. The next form, the next new thing, the next breakthrough idea, is probably rolling around in a young comedian's head, waiting to find its footing.

Where Chicago comedy is headed next is anyone's guess. But if history is bound to repeat itself, the next wave of comics will pull from Chicago's rich history. They'll take a piece from vaudeville, from the sick comics, from the intellectuals of the 1950s and from the boom of modern-day comedy.

EPILOGUE

C hicago has always been a playground for artists. After the Great Fire, the Chicago School of Architects came to practice its new form of building, the Art Institute continued to teach and host artists from all over the world and the mecca of comedy stomped its feet into the cement, making its mark forever. The lack of pretensions, media attention and money means that Chicago will always have the freedom to try and fail—and try again. And although Chicago will most likely always have its second city complex of wanting to play with the big boys, the overriding sense is that it doesn't care much whether it succeeds.

This most unlikeliest of cities, this "woman with a broken nose," this midwestern city that struggles to be a global contender, was born from the crazy ideas of a few and the willingness of millions to give it a try. Its destiny began with a connection that brought together the country; now, its fate lies in the hands of the people who pass through that connection. People are meant to pass through this city—some to stay and some to leave their marks here for someone else to pick up and experiment with.

What Chicago will create now will be anyone's guess, but whatever it is, the one thing for certain is that Chicago will continue to rub the lamps, fetch up the genii and give it a chance. If it fails, it will try again.

NOTES

CHAPTER 1

1. Chatfield-Taylor, *Chicago*, 118.
2. Pacyga, *Chicago*, 22.
3. Miller, *City of the Century*, 57.
4. Ibid., 44.
5. Peterson, "Founding Fathers," 19–23.
6. Andreas, *History of Chicago*, 472.

CHAPTER 2

1. Andreas, *History of Chicago*, 475.
2. Ibid., 476.
3. Samuelson interview.
4. Currey, *Chicago*, 244.
5. Andreas, *History of Chicago*, 489.
6. Ibid., 489.

CHAPTER 3

1. York, "Pursuit of Culture," 141–50.
2. Miller, *City of the Century*, 137.

3. Algren, *Chicago*, 11–12.
4. Samuelson interview.
5. *New York Times*, "Manager M'Vicker's Career."
6. Samuelson interview.

CHAPTER 4

1. *Chicago Tribune*, "Cheer Up."
2. Miller, *City of the Century*, 143
3. *Chicago Tribune*, "Cheer Up."
4. Andreas, *From the Fire*, 665.
5. Ogden to Wheeler, October 19, 1871.
6. Sandburg, *Chicago Poems*.

CHAPTER 5

1. *Theater*, January 8, 1908.

CHAPTER 6

1. Sherman, *Chicago Stage*, 221.
2. Samuelson interview.
3. Samuels and Samuels, *Once Upon a Stage*, 89.
4. Middleton, *Circus Memoirs*, 82.
5. Gehring, *Marx Brothers*, 18.
6. Samuelson interview.
7. Tucker, *Some of These Days*, 89.

CHAPTER 7

1. Samuelson interview.
2. Dunning, *On the Air*, 33.
3. Mcleod, *Original Amos 'n' Andy*.
4. Samuelson interview.
5. "Radio: The Chicago School."

6. Ibid.

7. Samuels, "Studs's Place."

8. "Radio: The Chicago School."

CHAPTER 8

1. Benny and Benny, *Sunday Nights at Seven*, 11.

2. Sanders, "Subversive Humor of Lenny Bruce."

3. "Nightclubs: The Sickniks."

4. "Obscenity Prosecutions of Lenny Bruce."

5. Bruce, *How to Talk Dirty*, 152.

6. Krassner, *Paul Krassner's Impolite Interviews*, 176.

7. Sweet, *Something Wonderful Right Away*, 128.

8. "Interview: Shelley Berman."

9. Weide, "Whyaduck Productions."

10. Haygood, "Pain and Passion of Dick Gregory."

11. Gregory and Moses. *Callous on My Soul*, 119.

12. Newhart, *I Shouldn't Be Doing This*, 7.

13. Ibid., 22.

14. Peabody Awards. "The Peabody Awards."

CHAPTER 9

1. Boyd, *Play and Game Theory.*

2. Review, *Film Quarterly.*

3. Spolin, *Improvisation for the Theater*, xlix.

4. "History of the Office, University of Chicago."

5. Samuelson interview.

6. Thomson and Sacks, *Cambridge Companion to Brecht.*

7. Sweet, *Something Wonderful Right Away*, 2.

8. Patinkin interview.

9. Ibid.

10. Johnson, *The Funniest in the Room*, 52–53.

11. Liebling, *Chicago*, 15.

12. Sahlins interview.

13. Ibid.

14. Johnson, *The Funniest in the Room*, 169.

15. Belushi, *Samurai Widow*, 43, 45.
16. Patinkin interview.

CHAPTER 10

1. Halpern interview.
2. Ibid.
3. Ibid.
4. Messing interview.
5. Fey interview.
6. Messing interview.
7. Halpern interview.
8. Ibid.

CHAPTER 11

1. Napier, "Annoyance Theatre & Bar."
2. Sutton interview.
3. Napier, "Annoyance Theatre & Bar."
4. Gaudet interview.
5. Ibid.
6. Hall interview.
7. Ibid.
8. Ibid.

CHAPTER 12

1. Haas interview.
2. Ibid.
3. Ibid.
4. Babylon interview.
5. Haas interview.
6. Babylon interview.

CHAPTER 13

1. Halpern interview.
2. Pitts interview.
3. Ibid.

BIBLIOGRAPHY

Algren, Nelson. *Chicago: City on the Make*. Garden City, NY: Doubleday, 1951.

"Amos and Andy | Old Time Radio." www.amosandandy.org.

Andreas, Alfred Theodore. *From the Fire of 1871 until 1885*. New York: Arno Press, 1975.

———. *History of Chicago from the Earliest Period to the Present Time*. Chicago: self-published, 1884.

Belushi, Judith Jacklin. *Samurai Widow*. New York: Carroll & Graf, 1990.

Benjamin, Rick. "DRAM: Notes for 'From Barrelhouse To Broadway: The Musical Odyssey Of Joe Jordan.'" www.dramonline.org.

Benny, Jack, and Joan Benny. *Sunday Nights at Seven: The Jack Benny Story*. New York: Warner Books, 1990.

Borrelli, Christopher. "Remembering 'Blues Brothers' 30 years later." *Chicago Tribune*, June 16, 2010.

Boyd, Neva Leona. *Play and Game Theory in Group Work: A Collection of Papers*. Chicago: Jane Addams Graduate School of Social Work, University of Illinois at Chicago Circle, 1971.

Brooker, Peter. "Key Words in Brecht's Theory and Practice of Theatre." In *The Cambridge Companion to Brecht*. Cambridge, UK: Cambridge University Press, 1994.

Bruce, Lenny. *How to Talk Dirty and Influence People: An Autobiography*. New York: Simon & Schuster, 1992.

Chatfield-Taylor, H.C. "The Soul of the City." In *Chicago*. Boston: Houghton Mifflin Co., 1917.

"The Chicago Crime Scenes Project." Chicago Crime Scenes Project. http://chicagocrimescenes.blogspot.com.

Chicago Tribune. "Cheer Up." October 11, 1871.

Currey, J. Seymour. Chicago: *Its History and Its Builders, A Century of Marvelous Growth.* Chicago: S.J. Clarke Pub. Co., 1912.

"Dick Gregory and Mort Sahl." 142 Throckmorton Theatre. www.142throckmortontheatre.com.

Dunning, John. *On the Air: The Encyclopedia of Old-Time Radio.* New York: Oxford University Press, 1998.

Encyclopedia of Arkansas History & Culture. www.encyclopediaofarkansas.net.

Encyclopedia of Chicago. http://encyclopedia.chicagohistory.org.

Gehring, Wes. *The Marx Brothers: A Bio-Bibliography.* Westport, CT: Greenwood Press, 1987.

Gregory, Dick, and Shelia P. Moses. *Callous on My Soul: A Memoir.* Atlanta, GA: Longstreet Press, 2000.

Haygood, Wil. "The Pain and Passion of Dick Gregory." *Boston Globe,* August 24, 2000.

History of Comedy. http://historyofcomedy.blogspot.com.

"History of the Office, Office of the President, The University of Chicago." http://president.uchicago.edu/history/hutchins.shtml.

"Interview: Shelley Berman." *Shecky.* www.sheckymagazine.com/berman.htm.

Jasen, David A. *Tin Pan Alley: An Encyclopedia of the Golden Age of American Song.* New York: Routledge, 2003.

Johnson, Kim. *The Funniest One in the Room: The Lives and Legends of Del Close.* Chicago: Chicago Review Press, 2008.

Kipling, Rudyard. *American Notes.* Charlottesville: University of Virginia Library, 1997.

Kozlowski, Rob. *The Art of Chicago Improv: Short Cuts to Long-Form Improvisation.* Portsmouth, NH: Heinemann, 2002.

Krassner, Paul. *Paul Krassner's Impolite Interviews.* New York: Seven Stories Press, 1999.

"Legal Opinions Relating to Obscenity Prosecutions of Comedian Lenny Bruce." UMKC School of Law. http://law2.umkc.edu/faculty/projects/ftrials/bruce/brucecourtdecisions.html.

Liebling, Joseph Abbott. *Chicago: The Second City.* New York: Alfred A. Knopf, 1952.

New York Times. "Manager M'Vicker's Career." March 9, 1896.

Mcleod, Elizabeth. *Original Amos 'n' Andy: Freeman Gosden, Charles Correll and the 1928–1943 Radio Serial.* Jefferson, NC: McFarland, 2009.

Middleton, *George. Circus Memoirs: Reminiscences of George Middleton as Told to and Written by His Wife*. Los Angeles: G. Rice & Sons, Printers, 1913.

Miller, Donald L. *City of the Century: The Epic of Chicago and the Making of America*. New York: Simon & Schuster, 1996.

Morgan, Thomas. "Jazz Roots: Shelton Brooks Discography." http://jass.com/sheltonbrooks/brooks.html.

Napier, Mick. "The Annoyance Theatre & Bar—History." The Annoyance Theatre & Bar, Plays, Musicals, Improv, Sketch Comedy & Improv Classes. www.annoyanceproductions.com/history/index.shtml.

Newhart, Bob. "Bob Newhart, 'I Shouldn't Even Be Doing This.'" NPR. www.npr.org/templates/transcript/transcript.php?storyId=6111083.

———. *I Shouldn't Even Be Doing This!: And Other Things that Strike Me as Funny*. New York: Hyperion, 2006.

"Nightclubs: The Sickniks." *Time*, July 13, 1959.

Pacyga, Dominic A. *Chicago: A Biography*. Chicago: University of Chicago Press, 2009.

Peabody Awards. "The Peabody Awards, An International Competition for Electronic Media, Honoring Achievement in Television, Radio, Cable and the Web, Administered by University of Georgia's Grady College of Journalism and Mass Communication." www.peabody.uga.edu/winners/details.php?id=904.

Peditto, Paul. "Dramatic Publishing." www.dramaticpublishing.com/AuthorsCorner.

Peterson, Jacqueline. "Founding Fathers: The Absorption of French-Indian Chicago" In *Ethnic Chicago*. Edited by Melvin G. Holli and Peter d'A. Jones. Grand Rapids, MI: W.B. Eerdmans Pub. Co., 1984.

Pierce, Bessie Louise, and Joe L. Norris, comps., eds. *As Others See Chicago: Impressions of Visitors, 1673–1933*. Chicago: University of Chicago Press, 1933.

"Radio: The Chicago School." *Time*, September 11, 1950.

Review. *Film Quarterly* (Fall/Winter 1963).

Samuels, Charles, and Louise Samuels. *Once Upon a Stage: The Merry World of Vaudeville*. New York: Dodd, Mead, 1974.

Samuels, Rich. "Studs's Place." Broadcasting in Chicago, 1921–1989. www.richsamuels.com/nbcmm/sp.html.

Sandburg, Carl. *Chicago Poems*. Raleigh, NC: Harcourt Brace, 1916.

Sanders, Barry. "The Subversive Humor of Lenny Bruce." Lecture, Chicago Humanities Festival, November 7, 2009.

Sherman, Robert L. *Chicago Stage, Its Records and Achievements*. Chicago: Robert L. Sherman, 1947.

Spolin, Viola. *Improvisation for the Theater: A Handbook of Teaching and Directing Techniques*. Evanston, IL: Northwestern University Press, 1963.

Sweet, Jeffrey. *Something Wonderful Right Away*. New York: Avon Books, 1978.

Theater, January 8, 1908.

Thomson, Peter, and Glendyr Sacks. *The Cambridge Companion to Brecht*. Cambridge, UK: Cambridge University Press, 1994.

Tucker, Sophie. *Some of These Days: The Autobiography of Sophie Tucker*. Garden City, NY: Doubleday, Doran and Co., 1945.

Twain, Mark. *Life on the Mississippi*. New York: Harper & Brothers, 1917.

"Vaudeville, A History." American Studies, University of Virginia. http://xroads.virginia.edu/~ma02/easton/vaudeville/vaudevillemain.html.

Weide, Robert. "Whyaduck Productions, Inc.—Dick Gregory: The Color of Funny." www.duckprods.com/projects/dickgregory.

West, Sandra L. *Encyclopedia of the Harlem Renaissance*. New York: Facts on File, Inc., 2003.

"Wicked, Immoral, Utterly Bad: The Many Stages of James McVicker." http://thelairoftheshadow.blogspot.com/2010/10/many-stages-of-james-mcvicker.html.

"World's Columbian Exposition: The Legacy of the Fair." American Studies, University of Virginia. http://xroads.virginia.edu/~ma96/wce/legacy.html.

York, Byron. "The Pursuit of Culture: Founding the Chicago Historical Society." *Chicago History* 10, no. 3 (Fall 1981): 141–50.

INTERVIEWS

Babylon, Brian. Interview by author. January 26, 2011.

Fey, Tina. Interview by Ed Zareh. August 11, 2009.

Gaudet, Dave. Interview by author. October 28, 2011.

Haas, Bert. Interview by author. November 20, 2011.

Hall, Don. Interview by author. November 14, 2011.

Halpern, Charna. Interview by author. January 6, 2011.

Messing, Susan. Interview by author. November 15, 2011.

Patinkin, Sheldon. Interview by author. January 11, 2011.

Pitts, Jonathan. Interview by author. January 24, 2011.

Sahlins, Bernie. Interview by author. November 3, 2011.

Samuelson, Tim. Interview by author. January 21, 2011.
Sloan, Joyce. Interview by author. May 2008.
Sutton, Mark. Interview by author. January 18, 2011.

INDEX

ABOUT THE AUTHOR

Margaret Hicks is a professional tour guide in Chicago who has been giving walking tours in the Loop (like her tour of Old Town offered through the famous Second City Comedy Club) since she completed the Chicago Architecture Foundation's docent program in 2004. She maintains her own website at www.chicagoelevated. com and has had years of experience in the Chicago comedy scene working at improv theaters and stand-up clubs.

Visit us at
www.historypress.net